CAMBRIDGE

Primary English

Workbook 3

Sarah Lindsay & Kate Ruttle

CAMBRIDGE
UNIVERSITY PRESS

University Printing House, Cambridge CB2 8BS, United Kingdom

One Liberty Plaza, 20th Floor, New York, NY 10006, USA

477 Williamstown Road, Port Melbourne, VIC 3207, Australia

314–321, 3rd Floor, Plot 3, Splendor Forum, Jasola District Centre, New Delhi – 110025, India

103 Penang Road, #05–06/07, Visioncrest Commercial, Singapore 238467

Cambridge University Press is part of the University of Cambridge.

It furthers the University's mission by disseminating knowledge in the pursuit of education, learning and research at the highest international levels of excellence.

www.cambridge.org
Information on this title: www.cambridge.org/9781108819558

© Cambridge University Press 2021

First published 2015
Second edition 2021

20 19 18 17 16 15 14 13 12 11 10 9 8 7 6 5

Printed in Italy by Rotolito S.p.A.

A catalogue record for this publication is available from the British Library

ISBN 978-1-108-81955-8 Paperback with Digital Access (1 Year)

Contents

> Acknowledgements

The authors and publishers acknowledge the following sources of copyright material and are grateful for the permissions granted. While every effort has been made, it has not always been possible to identify the sources of all the material used, or to trace all copyright holders. If any omissions are brought to our notice, we will be happy to include the appropriate acknowledgements on reprinting.

Unit 1 Excerpt from *Matilda* by Roald Dahl, text copyright 1988 by Roald Dahl. Used by permission of David Higham Associates and Viking Children's Books, an imprint of Penguin Young Readers Group, a division of Penguin Random House LLC. All rights reserved; **Unit 3** 'Dancing Poinciana' by Telecine Turner; **Unit 4** 'Bear and Fire' S.E Schlosser and AmericanFolklore.net. Copyright 2014. All rights reserved; Extracts from *Sinbad and the Roc* by Ian Whybrow, illustrated by Nick Schon, Cambridge Reading Adventures, Cambridge University Press, used by kind permission of the author; **Unit 6** Extract from *Four Clever Brothers* by Lynne Rickards, illustrated by Galia Bernstein © Cambridge University Press and UCL Institute of Education, 2017; **Unit 7** Extract and illustrations from *Alfie Small*: Pirates and Dragons by Nick Ward, copyright copyright by Nick Ward 2010, published by David Fickling Books 2012. Reprinted by permission of Penguin Books Limited; Extracts from *Dragon Boy* by Pippa Goodhart, illustrated by Martin Ursell, Reprinted by permission of HarperCollins Publishers Ltd, copyright 2003 Pippa Goodhart and Martin Ursell; **Unit 8** *Caribbean Islands* by Alice Harman, Wayland. Reproduced by permission of Wayland, an imprint of Hachette Children's Books;

Thanks to the following for permission to reproduce images:

Cover image by Pablo Gallego (Beehive Illustration); *Inside* **Unit 2** Monkeybusinessimages/GI; **Unit 3** kylewolfe/GI; **Unit 4** Chonticha Vatpongpee/GI; Prasngkh Ta Kha/GI; **Unit 5** Carol Yepes/GI; JakeOlimb/GI; Grafissimo/GI; Anton Petrus/GI; Alan Schein/GI; **Unit 6** Marji Lang/GI; **Unit 7** Image Source/GI; Wavebreakmedia/GI; fstop123/GI; Design Pics/GI; **Unit 8** SeanPavonePhoto/GI; onfilm/GI; simonbradfield/GI; TED MEAD/GI; Leisa Tyler/LightRocket/GI; thianchai sitthikongsak/GI; Debajyoti Chakraborty/NurPhoto/GI;

Key: GI= Getty Images

How to use this book

This Workbook provides questions for you to practise what you have learned in class. There is a unit to match each unit in your Learner's Book. There are six or twelve sessions in each unit and each session is divided into three parts:

Focus: these questions help you to master the basics ⟶

Practice: these questions help you to become more confident in using what you have learned ⟶

Challenge: these questions will make you think more ⟶ deeply

Focus

1 Finish these sentences using the correct words and phrases from these boxes.

| past | verb | doing, being or having | to be | present |

a A verb can be called a _____

   _____ word.

b A sentence must have a _____ in it.

c If something has already happened the verb is written in the

   _____ tense.

d If something is happening now the verb is written in the _____ tense.

e The most common verb in the English language is the verb

   _____ .

Practice

2 Write a character description of the boy.
   Give him a name. Think of things he may enjoy, like sport, music or fashion.

   _____

   _____

   _____

   _____

Challenge

3 Write each ou word in a sentence.

| should | could | our | your |
| would | out | you |

It is important to remember how to spell these *ou* words.

We must wash <u>our</u> hands before we eat lunch.

   _____

   _____

1 ▶ Story writing with Roald Dahl

❯ 1.1 Setting the scene

> **Language focus**
>
> **Nouns** are words we use to name things.
>
> Examples: *house, bed, shop, beach, hill, flower*
>
> **Adjectives** are words we use to describe nouns.
>
> Examples: *big, small, pretty, lovely, nice, dirty, horrible, high, low*

Focus

1 Look at these words. <u>Underline</u> the **nouns** and ⭕circle the **adjectives**.

mountain	butterfly	book
interesting	beautiful	office
rabbit	young	happy
clever	shirt	rain
sharp	blue	computer

Practice

2 List six different settings. Next to each setting write a noun and adjective that are linked to it.

a beach _____ _____

_____ _____ _____

‾‾‾‾‾‾‾‾‾‾‾   ‾‾‾‾‾‾‾‾‾‾‾   ‾‾‾‾‾‾‾‾‾‾‾

‾‾‾‾‾‾‾‾‾‾‾   ‾‾‾‾‾‾‾‾‾‾‾   ‾‾‾‾‾‾‾‾‾‾‾

‾‾‾‾‾‾‾‾‾‾‾   ‾‾‾‾‾‾‾‾‾‾‾   ‾‾‾‾‾‾‾‾‾‾‾

‾‾‾‾‾‾‾‾‾‾‾   ‾‾‾‾‾‾‾‾‾‾‾   ‾‾‾‾‾‾‾‾‾‾‾

Challenge

3   Stick or draw a picture of a setting in the box.

Label at least six different things in the picture.
Use an adjective and a noun in each label.

For example: blue sky, white clouds

> 1.2 Looking at a setting

Focus

1 Carefully read through the setting of Miss Honey's cottage from *Matilda*. Circle all the nouns you can find.

> **Miss Honey's Home**
>
> The bricks it was built of were old and crumbly and very pale red. It had a slate roof and one small chimney, and there were two little windows at the front. Each window was no larger than a sheet of newspaper and there was clearly no upstairs to the place. On either side of the path there was a wilderness of nettles and thorns and long brown grass.
>
> *Roald Dahl*

Practice

2 List the adjectives used in the setting above.

Challenge

3   Draw a line to match the vocabulary with its meaning.
    You could use a different colour pencil for each line.

human dwelling   a wild area

slate   to hold something closely

wilderness   very big, huge

embracing   a grey rock used to make a roof

enormous   a place where people live

> 1.3 Build a picture with words

Focus

1   Write another *ou* word that rhymes with each of these words.

    house _____   round _____

    would _____   mouth _____

    loud   _____

Practice

2   Sort these ou words into the correct columns in the table.

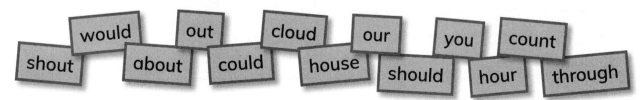

would   out   cloud   our   you   count
shout   about   could   house   should   hour   through

When ou sounds like the oo in stood	When ou sounds like the ou in mouse	When ou sounds like the oo in too	When ou sounds like the ow in cow

Challenge

3 Write each ou word in a sentence.

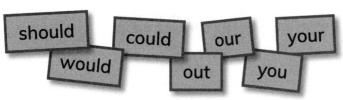

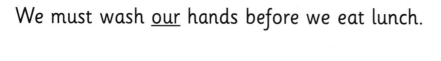

It is important to remember how to spell these *ou* words.

We must wash <u>our</u> hands before we eat lunch.

_____

_____

_____

_____

_____

_____

> 1.4 Writing a setting

Focus

Picture A

Picture B

Look at the two pictures of a car park near a shopping mall.

1 Think about the things that are the same and the things that are different in these pictures.

2 List four different adjectives that could describe each picture.

Picture A   **Picture B**

_____   _____

_____   _____

_____   _____

_____   _____

Practice

3 Look again at the pictures. Add words to the gaps to finish these descriptions.

Make your descriptions as interesting as possible.

11 >

Picture A

It is a _____ day. The sky is _____ so everyone feels

_____ . Some people are arriving. They are feeling _____ as

they walk towards the mall. Others have spent a _____ time in the

shops. They look _____ as they walk back to their cars.

Picture B

It is a _____ day. There is a _____ storm. The sky is

_____ so everyone feels _____ . The people who are arriving

are feeling _____ as they walk towards the mall. Other people are

leaving. They look _____ as they hurry back to their cars.

Challenge

4 Read this description. Then improve it by choosing a more descriptive
   word to replace the eight words in **bold**. Try to use a different word
   each time. Write your words in the spaces below.

> It was a **nice** day so we decided to go to the beach. I was feeling **happy**.
> The beach was **nice** and all the people were **happy**. I wanted to paddle
> in the sea. The water felt **nice**. After my paddle, I had a **nice** ice cream.
> 'I am **happy**,' I told my mum. 'Thank you for such a **nice** day out.'

_____   _____

_____   _____

_____   _____

› 1.5 Looking at characters

Focus

1 List as many adjectives as you can that describe this boy.

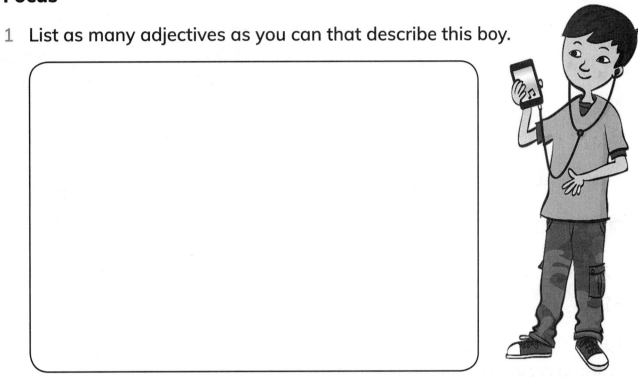

Practice

2 Write a character description of the boy.

Give him a name. Think of things he may enjoy, like sport, music or fashion.

_____

_____

_____

_____

_____

Challenge

3 Match the adjectives on the left with the adjectives on the right that mean nearly the same thing.

friendly   enthusiastic

happy   occupied

kind   delighted

busy   welcoming

interested   considerate

excited   engrossed

You may need to use a dictionary or a thesaurus.

> ## 1.6 What happens next?

Focus

1 We are going to look at the words used in *The Enormous Crocodile*.

Look at this word web for the word *enormous*.

Finish the word web by adding the words from the boxes.

small   big   huge   gigantic   tiny   little

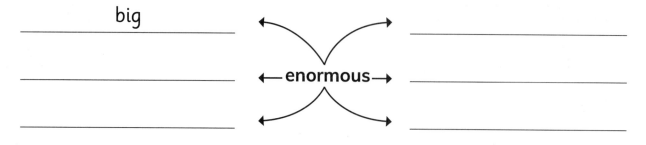

Words that mean the same   **Words that mean the opposite**

big

←enormous→

Practice

2   Add your own words to this word web.

Words that mean the same   **Words that mean the opposite**

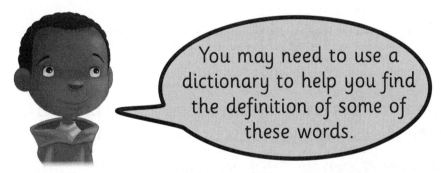

_____   _____

_____   ← brave →   _____

_____   _____

Challenge

3   Write your own definition for each of these words.

You may need to use a dictionary to help you find the definition of some of these words.

crocodile: a large, scaly reptile with short legs and large, strong jaws

lunch: _____

sharp: _____

gulp: _____

bitter: _____

greedy: _____

jungle: _____

secret: _____

> 1.7 Looking at verbs

Language focus

Verbs tell you what someone or something *does, is* or *has*. Verbs are sometimes called *doing* words, but they are also *being* or *having* words.

Verbs also tell you **when** the action in the sentence happens.

What?	When?	Tense
He **walked** to school.	Has already happened	past
She **walks** to school.	Is happening now	present

The verb *to be* is the most common verb in the English language. Different parts of the verb are tricky to recognise. They include the little words am, is, are, was and were.

Focus

1 Finish these sentences using the correct words and phrases from these boxes.

| past | verb | doing, being or having | to be | present |

a A verb can be called a _____

_____ word.

b A sentence must have a _____ in it.

c If something has already happened the verb is written in the

_____ tense.

d If something is happening now the verb is written in the _____ tense.

e The most common verb in the English language is the verb

_____ .

Practice

2 Look at the sentences. Are they in the past or present tense?

Underline the verb in the sentences. Then write *past* or *present* for each sentence. The first one has been done for you.

a He <u>had</u> a cup of chai after school.   _____past_____

b The phone rings all day long.   _____

c We are all here today.   _____

d The baby owls learned to fly.   _____

e Hidaya picked her friends for her cricket team.   _____

f The tree outside my window grows very fast.   _____

Challenge

3 Look at these groups of words.
Circle the forms of the verb *to be* in each triangle.

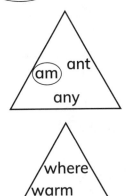
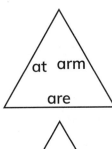
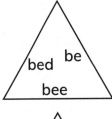
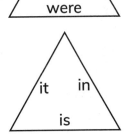
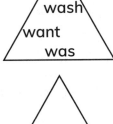

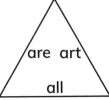
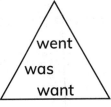

> 1.8 Speech in texts

> **Language focus**
>
> **Speech marks** are placed around the words that are said by a character.
>
> **Example:** 'Is it lunch time?' asked the Enormous Crocodile.

Focus

1 Read this short extract.

   a Using a coloured pencil, <u>underline</u> the words that Miho said.

   b Using a different coloured pencil, <u>underline</u> the words that her son Yuu said.

> 'Where are you going?' shrieked Miho, as Yuu ran off.
>
> Yuu looked over his shoulder and shouted, 'I'll be back later, mother.'
>
> Much later, when Yuu came home, his mother was waiting for him. 'Where have you been?' she demanded. 'I have been so worried!'
>
> 'I'm sorry,' mumbled Yuu. 'I had forgotten to do something important, but then I remembered it.'
>
> 'Nothing is that important,' complained Miho. 'Boys should do what their mother tells them to do.'
>
> 'But this was very important!' declared Yuu. 'I had forgotten to get your present. But then I remembered. Look!' He held out a small box.
>
> 'You are a good boy!' stated Miho, giving Yuu a kiss and rubbing his head.

Practice

2   List all the dialogue verbs in the extract that could be replaced by *said*.

_____

_____

_____

Challenge

3   Continue the dialogue in the extract.

Write two sentences. One said by Yuu, the other by Miho.

_____

_____

_____

_____

Remember to include interesting dialogue verbs in your extra sentences.

> 1.9 Sequencing events

Focus

1 Choose a story you know.

Decide on the six main ideas or events in the story and write them on the story mountain.

Title: _____

Author: _____

3 Development	4 Exciting part

2 Beginning/Problem	5 Then what happens?

1 Introduction	6 Ending

Practice

2 Answer these questions about your chosen story.

   a Who is the main character in the story?

_____

   b Write three adjectives to describe the main character.

_____   _____   _____

   c Who are the other important characters?

_____

_____

   d Where is the story set?

_____

   e Write three adjectives to describe the setting.

_____   _____   _____

Challenge

3 Write your own character or setting description from the story.

_____

_____

_____

_____

> 1.10 Planning a story

Focus

1 Plan a story.

Think about what might happen in the beginning, the middle and the end of the story.

Make notes.

> The beginning

> The middle

> The end

Practice

2 Think about the characters and settings for your story.

Write words or draw pictures in the boxes.

Characters

Settings

Challenge

3 Add your story ideas to the story mountain.

3 Development		4 Exciting part

2 Beginning/Problem		5 Then what happens?

1 Introduction		6 Ending

> 1.11 Writing a story

Focus

1   The writer of this story has forgotten some of the capital letters and full stops.

Make the following corrections to the story.

   a   Change four letters to capital letters.

   b   Add the five missing full stops.

> Marco loved riding his bike but he was getting too big for it he needed a new bike but he knew his papa didn't have enough money one day he saw a notice for a bike race the prize was a new bike marco wanted that new bike but first he would have to win the race on his little bike

Practice

2   Complete the following spelling log.

It's easy to forget the correct spelling of words when you write a story.

Word	Difficult bit	Word	Similar word	Similar word
was	wa	was	want	
said	ai		again	
there	ere			

Challenge

3   Choose five words from your writing that are difficult to spell.

Write them in the first column of the spelling log and then finish the log.

Word	Difficult bit	Word	Similar word	Similar word

> 1.12 Improving your story

Focus

1   Add words to these sentences to make them more interesting.

a   The man walked into the shop.

The tired, old man shuffled into the noisy shop.

b   The dog ran off towards the beach.

c A girl climbed up to the top of the slide.

_____

_____

d The park was full of children.

_____

_____

e The bedroom was a mess.

_____

_____

Practice

2 Look at this picture. Make up an interesting conversation between the two characters.

You can change and add as many words as you like.

Remember not to use the dialogue word *said* too many times.

_____

_____

_____

_____

_____

_____

Challenge

3 Proofread this paragraph. Mark your corrections on the paragraph.
Check:

- grammar   • spelling   • punctuation.

'Where are we going?' asked anja.

Shall we going back to my house to make some sweets? Jonah replied.

Jonah had just remember it were his grandmother's birthday the next

day. he wanted to make somthing for her.

Wat a great idea, laughed Anja. I could make some sweets for my

bruther too, it was his birthday next week.

It is always a good idea to proofread your writing, just in case you have made any small errors.

2 Let's have a party

> 2.1 Looking at celebrations

Focus

1   Write all the words you think of when you hear the word *celebration*.

Practice

This is a definition of the word *celebration* found in a dictionary.

Dictionary	Definition
celebration	a happy event marking an occasion, e.g. birthday party

Remember that *e.g.* means *for example*

2 Write definitions for each of these words. Use a dictionary to help you.

a **ceremony** _____

b **festival** _____

c **anniversary** _____

d **fiesta** _____

e **carnival** _____

Challenge

3 There are 20 words in this wordsearch.
All the words are linked to celebrations!

The words can go across or down. Count how many you can find.

F	A	M	I	L	Y	E	H	A	P	P	Y
R	B	O	L	I	P	A	R	A	D	E	S
A	N	N	I	V	E	R	S	A	R	Y	M
N	T	H	E	G	R	E	O	N	U	F	E
T	F	F	L	A	F	T	R	N	M	I	A
C	E	R	E	M	O	N	Y	I	S	E	L
P	S	I	T	E	R	A	F	E	A	S	T
A	T	E	E	S	M	E	E	T	I	T	G
R	I	N	F	C	A	R	N	I	V	A	L
T	V	D	U	I	N	K	J	H	U	N	A
Y	A	S	N	N	C	J	O	L	L	Y	U
A	L	W	F	T	E	N	Y	O	D	O	G
B	I	R	T	H	D	A	Y	Z	I	N	H

anniversary   fun

birthday   games

carnival   happy

ceremony   jolly

enjoy   laugh

family   meal

feast   meet

festival   parade

fiesta   party

friends   performance

› 2.2 Writing lists

Focus

1 Write in the thought bubbles all the things you need to do before having a party.

Write them in note form.

Practice

2 If you are inviting someone to a party, what information do they
need to know? Write a list.

_____   _____

_____   _____

_____   _____

Challenge

3 Write verbs that describe things you could do at a party.
List as many as you can.

dance   talk

> 2.3 Fiction or non-fiction?

Focus

1   Write a definition for these text types.

    a   **fiction**   _____

    b   **non-fiction**   _____

2   Write a book title for each of these text-types.
    These can be made up or real book titles.

    a   **fiction**   _____

    b   **non-fiction**   _____

Practice

3   Read this text and answer
    the questions.

    a   Is this text fiction or
        non-fiction?

        _____

        _____

        _____

        _____

Amelia

You are invited to:
Vovó's Surprise Party.

It will be at: Santa
Teresa Colombo
Café,

Rio de Janeiro

On: 18 May at 4.30.

Come dressed to
impress.

RSVP

b Which three features help you to answer Question a?

Feature 1: _____

Feature 2: _____

Feature 3: _____

c Why has someone written this text?

_____

d Who would read this text?

_____

e What type of text is it?

_____

Challenge

4 Read this text and answer the questions.

How to make a sponge cake

You will need:
- 175 g softened butter, sugar and flour
- 3 medium eggs
- 1 tsp baking powder

What to do:
1 First, mix together the butter and the sugar.
2 Add the eggs and beat until smooth and creamy.
3 Now, mix the baking powder in with the flour.
4 Then, sift the flour into the butter mix and gently mix in.
5 Finally, spoon the mixture into two shallow cake tins and bake in a medium oven for 25 minutes.
6 When the cake is cool, decorate it with sweets and coloured icing.

a   Is this text fiction or non-fiction?

_____

b   Which three features help you to answer Question a?

Feature 1:   _____

Feature 2:   _____

Feature 3:   _____

c   Why has someone written this text?

_____

d   Who would read this text?

_____

e   What type of text is it?

_____

> 2.4 Following instructions

Language focus

The form of the verb used in instruction texts is sometimes called a **command** or **imperative verb** because it tells, or commands, you to do something, such as draw, open or fold. It is a 'bossy' verb.

Words such as first, next and finally tell you the order to do things in. They are called **sequencing words.**

Instructions usually begin with a command verb or a sequencing word.

Focus

1 Look at the recipe for salt dough.

a Use a coloured pencil to (circle) all the verbs.

b <u>Underline</u> the sequencing words.

How to make salt dough

You need:

- 2 cups of flour
- 1 cup of salt
- 1 cup of warm water
- a cup for measuring
- a large mixing bowl
- a spoon
- an airtight container

What to do:

1 Mix together the flour and salt in a large bowl.

2 Then, slowly stir in the warm water.

3 Mix well until the mixture feels like dough.

4 Use your hands to push the mixture into a ball.

5 Knead for at least five minutes or until smooth.

6 Finally, put the salt dough in an airtight container to keep it soft.

Practice

2 Order the words to give the instructions for making a pop-up card.

> If you make your own salt dough, it will keep for up to a week in an airtight container.

   a   the / first / in / card / half / fold

_____

   b   fold / card / next / small / the

_____

   c   stick / big / card / the / small / into / card / the

_____

   d   a / draw / picture / then

_____

   e   the / on / picture / the / card / stick / small / finally

_____

> Remember, look for command verbs or sequencing words to start each line, and remember to use capital letters and full stops!

Challenge

3 Write three things that tell you that **How to make salt dough** and **How to make a pop-up card** are instruction texts.

_____

_____

_____

› 2.5 Writing an invitation

> **Language focus**
>
> Before adding *–ing* or *–ed* to a word, look at *the letter before the last letter* to see if it is a **consonant** or a **vowel**.
>
> - If it is a **consonant**, just add *–ing* or *–ed*, but if the last letter is an e, remove the e before adding *–ing* or *–ed*.
>
>   **Example:** call = calling   invite = inviting
>
> - If it is a **single vowel**, just double the last letter before adding *–ing* or *–ed*, but don't double the last letter if the word ends in w, x or y.
>
>   **Example:** stir = stirring   play = playing
>
> - If there are two vowel letters, just add *–ing* or *–ed*.
>
>   **Example:** beep = beeping

Focus

1   All these words have either one consonant or a double vowel before the last letter.

Finish the word sums.

a   land + –ing = _____   d   read + –ing = _____

b   stoop + –ed = _____   e   help + –ed   = _____

c   bump + –ing = _____   f   meet + –ing = _____

2   Complete the rule.

When adding *–ing* or *–ed* to words that have either one consonant

or two vowel letters before the last letter _____

_____

_____

Practice

3 Add –ing to each of these words.

Think carefully about any changes that need to be made to the words before you add –ing.

a tune + –ing = _____   f skate + –ing = _____

b bury + –ing = _____   g tow + –ing = _____

c flap + –ing = _____   h rub + –ing = _____

d tip + –ing = _____   i behave + –ing = _____

e save + –ing = _____

Challenge

4 Underline the verb or verbs in these sentences. Then rewrite the sentences in the past tense by adding –ed to the verbs.

a Taila plans a party.

Taila planned a party.

b She invites all her friends.

_____

c She wants to play lots of games.

_____

d She cooks some lovely food.

_____

e Her friends arrive.

_____

f She dances with her friends.

_____

› 2.6 Following and writing instructions

Focus

1 Tick (✓) the sentences that come from an instruction text.

   a Then walk to the traffic lights. ☐

   b It is not a good idea to push people in the playground. ☐

   c Be kind to each other. ☐

   d Turn left after the letterbox. ☐

   e I made a cake yesterday. First, I went and bought some flour. ☐

   f Add the milk and stir. ☐

Practice

2 Look carefully at these words. Copy the compound words.

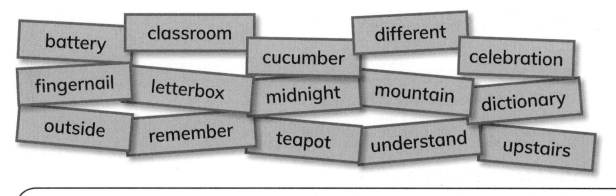

battery   classroom   cucumber   different   celebration
fingernail   letterbox   midnight   mountain   dictionary
outside   remember   teapot   understand   upstairs

Challenge

3 Write three sentences.

Each sentence must be an instruction and include a compound word.

Sentence 1: _____

Sentence 2: _____

Sentence 3: _____

> 2.7 Contents pages and indexes

Text A

Healthy drinks

Nutty banana whirl	28
Orange refresher	28
Honey and yoghurt smoothie	29

Healthy snacks

Fruit rockets	31
Orange oat biscuits	32
Carrot slice	33

Text B

apple 27, 35	melon 31
apricots 16, 21, 26	milk 24, 28
banana 24, 28, 31	nuts 17, 28, 35
butter 13, 32, 33, 34	oats 16, 26, 32
carrot 33	orange 6, 17, 28, 29
flour 19, 23, 32, 22	orange juice 28
honey 15, 21, 28, 29	pineapple 31
jelly 17, 26, 35	strawberry 31, 34
lemon 16, 23, 25	sugar 16, 33, 37
lemon juice 28	watermelon 31

Focus

1 Look at Text A and Text B. Then answer these questions.

a Which text (A or B) shows a contents page?

_____

b What is the other text?

_____

c Where would you find Text A: at the beginning, in the middle or at the end of a book?

_____

d Where would you find Text B: at the beginning, in the middle or at the end of a book?

_____

e What type of book do these pages come from?

_____

Practice

2   Now answer these questions.

    a   Which two healthy drinks would you find on page 28?

    _____

    b   Which page would you go to if you wanted to make fruit rockets?

    _____

    c   Which three pages have recipes that use bananas?

    _____

    d   Which page has a recipe that uses pineapple?

    _____

    e   Which three ingredients do we know can be found in the carrot slice?

    _____

Challenge

3   Finally, answer these questions.

    a   Do you think Text A shows the whole Contents page?

    _____

    b   Why? Give two reasons for your answer.

    Reason 1: _____

    _____

    Reason 2: _____

    _____

> 2.8 Making lists

Focus

1 Write a list of your eight favourite types of food.

_____   _____

_____   _____

_____   _____

_____   _____

Practice

2 Now rewrite the list in alphabetical order, as if they were in an index.

Remember
your alphabet:
a b c d e f g h i
j k l m n o p q r
s t u v w x y z

_____

_____

_____

_____

_____

Challenge

3 Imagine you are having your own party.
Write a list of everyone you would like to invite.

› 2.9 Giving instructions

Focus

1 Draw a picture of a game you enjoy playing at parties.

Label the things you need for the game.

Practice

2 Write notes about how the game is played. Think carefully about the important information you need to tell your friends when playing this game.

_____

_____

_____

_____

_____

_____

Challenge

3 Practise saying aloud the instructions for the game.

Have you remembered all the key information?

Try giving the instructions to friends or family before playing the game with them.

› 2.10 Planning a game

Focus

1 The instructions of **How to play Fruit Basket** have been muddled up.

Write a number from 1–7 next to each instruction to show the correct order.

The order of some instructions will be more important than others.

☐ Choose one player to stand in the middle of the circle.

☐ Divide 9 players into groups of three.

☐ If the player in the middle wants to do something different, they can call out 'Fruit basket!' That means everyone has to find a new position in the circle.

☐ Mix the players up and place the players in a circle around a central point.

☐ When the game finishes, you do not want to be the one in the middle!

☐ The player in the middle then calls out the name of one of the groups, for example, 'Pineapple!' Everyone in that group must now move to a different place as quickly as they can. The player who is the last to a place now has to stand in the middle of the circle.

☐ Name each group a type of fruit, for example, *banana, pineapple*.

Practice

2 Write three tips for what to include when writing instructions.

Tip 1: _____

Tip 2: _____

Tip 3: _____

Challenge

3 Improve each of these instructions. Make them shorter.

 a If the player in the middle wanted to do something different they could call out 'Fruit basket!' That means everyone has to find a new position in the circle.

_____

_____

 b The player in the middle then calls out the name of one of the groups, for example, 'Pineapple!' Everyone in that group must now move to a different place as quickly as they can. The player last to a place now has to stand in the middle of the circle.

_____

_____

> 2.11 Writing instructions

Focus

1 Pretend you are a teacher. Read the instructions for this game.

Well, you all need to sit in a circle.
Everyone has to be quiet.
You need to get your paper mouse.
Everyone puts their mouse in the middle of the circle and holds on to their mouse's tail.
I have the cone.
I will bang the cone down on the mouse.
Everyone needs to try to pull their mouse out the way.

a What has the writer done well?

_____

b Is there anything that could be improved?

_____

c Write notes on the instructions or on a separate piece of paper to give the writer feedback.

Practice

2 Rewrite the instructions for the game.

- Correct any mistakes you found.
- Use the feedback you gave in **Focus** to help you.

_____

_____

_____

_____

_____

_____

Challenge

3 Write instructions for a playground game you know on the next page.

- Keep the instructions short, simple and in the correct order.
- Remember to include command verbs and sequencing words.

_____

_____

_____

_____

_____

_____

_____

〉 2.12 Improving your instructions

Focus

1 Think about why we write instructions. Answer these questions.

a What have you learned about instructions? Write three things.

_____

_____

_____

b Why are instructions useful when you are planning your party?

_____

_____

Practice

2   Read this text. Use the information to complete the invitation.

From: Sonia.sabell@lemail.com
To: Mbeke@baschools.arg
Subject: birthday party

I saw Lisha today. She said that she was going to invite Mbeke to her birthday party on 18th November. Lisha said that her party will be at the New Club on Ikwere Road.
It sounds like it will be a great party because everyone has to go dressed as an animal!
Lisha wants everyone to have some of her birthday cake.

So she's having the party from 3 pm until 5 pm.

Dear
_____

You are invited to
_____
_____
_____
_____

It will be at
_____
_____
_____

on _____
at _____

Challenge

3 Look at the map. Write instructions for Mbeke describing how she will get from her house to the party at New Club.

_____

_____

_____

_____

_____

3 ▶ Poems from around the world

> 3.1 Words that make pictures

Read the poem and answer the questions.

Dancing Poinciana

Fire in the treetops,

Fire in the sky.

Blossoms red as sunset

Dazzling to the eye.

Dance, Poinciana,

Sway, Poinciana,

On a sea of green.

Dance, Poinciana,

Sway, Poinciana,

Regal as a queen.

Fire in the treetops,

Fire in the sky.

Crimson petals and white

Stained with scarlet dye.

Dance, Poinciana,

Sway, Poinciana,

On a sea of green.

Dance, Poinciana,

Sway, Poinciana,

Regal as a queen.

Telcine Turner

Focus

1 What colour are the flowers on the tree? _____

2 Do you think the poem is about a fire? Why?

   _____

   _____

3 Write a word from the poem that rhymes with dye. _____

4 What does the word *regal* mean? Tick (✓) the best answer.

   a real   ☐

   b red   ☐

   c funny   ☐

   d noble   ☐

Practice

5 What does 'On a sea of green' describe?

   _____

6 What sort of weather is being described in the poem?
   Tick (✓) the best answer.

   a no wind   ☐

   b a gentle breeze   ☐

   c a storm   ☐

   d a hurricane   ☐

7 Explain your answer to Question 6.

_____

_____

8 Which words suggest the movement the tree makes?

_____   _____

Challenge

9 Write a short review of this poem. Include:

- what the poem is about
- which country it represents
- who wrote it
- what you thought about it
- whether you would recommend it to others.

_____

_____

_____

_____

_____

_____

_____

> 3.2 Reading with expression

Language focus

- For most **verbs**, just add –ing to the end of the verb.
- For verbs that end in e, take off the e and then add –ing.
- For verbs that have a short vowel followed by one consonant, double the consonant and then add –ing.

Focus

1 How quickly can you <u>underline</u> all the –ing forms of verbs in this text? Time yourself!

Then check you haven't missed any.

The king was counting his gold. 'Bring me more gold!' he shouted.

His soldiers went running into the town. They saw children skipping and laughing, and the soldiers shouted to them, 'Bring us your gold, your rings and your coins. The king needs more gold!'

Some people were standing nearby, looking at a pile of old clothes. They stopped looking and stood staring at the soldiers, not believing what they had just heard. Suddenly, everyone saw the pile of old clothes was standing up and it was talking.

'No!' said the pile of old clothes, which was really a very old man. 'The king has been spending too much money too quickly. He must learn to save his money, not spend it.'

So without giving the soldiers anything, the people went back into their houses, the parents carrying their children. And instead of running around, the soldiers walked slowly back to the palace to see the king. They told him what the very old man had said.

When they had finished telling their tale, the soldiers saw that the king was weeping. Tears were flowing down his cheeks, but he was smiling. 'Bring the very old man to me,' he said. 'He is wise and I need his help.'

Practice

2 Complete the lists of verbs and –ing forms.

smile	→	_____		_____	→	coming
say	→	_____	dance	→	_____
_____	→	going	howl	→	_____
run	→	_____		_____	→	staring
drop	→	_____	fly	→	_____
_____	→	walking		_____	→	pulling
like	→	_____		_____	→	flashing
_____	→	standing	hurry	→	_____
_____	→	rushing		_____	→	roaring
clap	→	_____	become	→	_____

Challenge

3 Write three sentences about a hurricane, each with two verbs using the –ing suffix.

Sentence 1: _____

Sentence 2: _____

Sentence 3: _____

> 3.3 Performing a poem

Language focus

A **noun phrase** is a group of words that are used instead of a noun.

A noun phrase can be replaced by a pronoun.

his huge, leathery wings   →   they

         noun phrase   pronoun

Notice how adjectives describe the noun in this noun phrase.

Focus

1 <u>Underline</u> the noun phrase that includes adjectives in each of these sentences.

   a   The huge, scaly dragon flew high above the mountain.

   b   People stood and watched as the bright swords of light shot through the clouds.

   c   A dragon crashed two large, shiny stones together.

   d   The people shelter from the thunder and lightning in a dark, smelly cave.

   e   At last the dragon flies over the tall mountain range to another area.

Practice

2 Rewrite these sentences swapping the noun phrases, which you underlined above, for pronouns.

   a   The huge, scaly dragon flew high above the mountain.

      It flew high above the mountain.

b People stood and watched as the bright swords of light shot
   through the clouds.

   _____

   _____

c A dragon crashed two large, shiny stones together.

   _____

   _____

d The people shelter from the thunder and lightning in a dark,
   smelly cave.

   _____

   _____

e At last the dragon flies over the tall mountain range to another area.

   _____

   _____

Challenge

3 Write a noun phrase using adjectives for each of these nouns.

   a water   _____

   b fire   _____

   c thunder _____

   d clothes _____

   e weather _____

> 3.4 Onomatopoeia

Language focus

Onomatopoeia is when a word mimics or describes a sound of the object or action it is about. Onomatopoeia can bring a poem to life, as it has done in *Song of the Animal World*.

Example:	Narrator:	The fish goes
	Chorus:	Plop!
	Narrator:	The bird goes
	Chorus:	Cheep!
	Narrator:	The monkey goes
	Chorus:	Screech!

Other examples of onomatopoeia are slither, rustle, bang and buzz.

Focus

1 With a line, match the animals with the sounds they make.

cluck

growl

hiss

hee-haw

meow

Practice

2   Write each of these onomatopoeic words into a sentence
about an animal.

screech   _____

squeak   _____

twitter   _____

bleat   _____

Challenge

Read the poem and answer the questions.

Song of the Animal World

Narrator: The fish goes

Chorus: Plop!

Narrator: The bird goes

Chorus: Cheep!

Narrator: The monkey goes

Chorus: Screech!

Fish: I start to the left,
I twist to the right.
I am the fish
That slips through the water,
That slides,
That twists,
That leaps!

Narrator: Everything lives,
Everything dances,
Everything sings.

Chorus: Plop! Cheep! Screech!

Bird: The bird flies away,
Flies, flies, flies,
Goes, returns, passes,
Climbs, floats, swoops.
I am the bird!

Narrator: Everything lives,
Everything dances,
Everything sings.

Chorus: Plop! Cheep! Screech!

> **Monkey:** The monkey!
> From branch to branch
> Runs, hops, jumps,
> With his wife and baby,
> Mouth stuffed full, tail in air,
> Here's the monkey!
> Here's the monkey!
>
> **Narrator:** Everything lives,
> Everything dances,
> Everything sings.
> **Chorus:** Plop! Cheep! Screech!
>
> *Traditional*

3 Which creature goes Cheep?

_____

4 What do you think the word Cheep describes? Tick (✓) the best answer.

   a the sound the animal makes when it eats ⬜

   b the sound the animal makes when it is angry ⬜

   c the sound the animal makes when it sings ⬜

   d the sound the animal makes when it sleeps ⬜

5 Which way does the fish move first?

_____

6 Write another word from the poem that means the same as *slips*.

_____

7 Write an onomatopoeic word from the poem linked to the monkey.

_____

8 Write your own word which might describe how the bird comes back down once it has flown up high?

_____

⟩ 3.5 Writing a haiku

Language focus

The number of **syllables** in a word helps give it rhythm.

Examples:

- The word cat has one syllable.
- Awake (a-wake) has two syllables and so does stretching (stre-tching).
- Suddenly (sud-den-ly) has three syllables – and so does syllables (syl-la-bles)!

Focus

1   Write the number of syllables in each line of this haiku.

> Suddenly awake.   _____
>
> Stretching, yawning, arching back,   _____
>
> stalking, pouncing: cat.   _____

Practice

2   Choose an animal.

   a   Write four powerful verbs about what the animal does.

   b   Next to each word, write the number of syllables it has.

    _____ _____   _____ _____

    _____ _____   _____ _____

3   Write four powerful nouns or noun phrases about what the animal
    you chose looks like. Next to each word/phrase write the number of
    syllables it has.

    _____ _____ _____ _____

    _____ _____ _____ _____

    _____ _____ _____ _____

4   Write something the animal does that is unusual.
    Write the number of syllables this word/phrase has.

    _____ _____

    _____ _____

    _____ _____

Challenge

5   Use the words and phrases from **Practice** to write your
    Haiku about your chosen animal. Give your haiku a title.

    _____

    _____

    _____

> **Tip**
>
> Remember, haikus are poems with 17 syllables and three lines. There
> are five syllables in the first and last lines, and seven syllables in the
> middle line. Haikus are very short but you should still be able to see a
> clear picture of the subject in your head when you read them.

❭ 3.6 Reviewing poems

Choose a poem you enjoy, then complete the activities.

Focus

1 Write a short summary of the poem.

Include:

- the poem title
- who wrote it
- which country it might be from
- a few sentences describing what the poem is about.

Practice

2 Now write about the structure of the poem.
- Does it rhyme?
- How many lines does it have?
- Are there any patterns in the structure of the poem?

Challenge

3 Finally, write your own version of the poem or a verse of the poem.

Remember to:

- use the same patterns of sound and language
- use the same number of lines
- use the same kind of words.

4 ▶ Myths and legends

⟩ 4.1 Looking at a traditional story

Read the myth *Bear and Fire* then answer the questions.

Bear and Fire

In the beginning, Bear owned Fire. Fire warmed Bear and his people on cold days and it gave them light when the nights were long and dark. Bear always carried Fire with him. One day, Bear and his people went to a forest. Bear put Fire down at the edge of the forest, then Bear and his people went deeper and deeper into the forest to look for food. Fire blazed up happily for a while until it had burned nearly all of its wood. It started to smoke and flicker, then it dwindled down and down. Fire was worried. It was nearly out. 'Feed me! Feed me!' shouted Fire. But Bear and his people had wandered deep into the forest, and they did not hear Fire's cries. At that moment, Man came walking through the forest and saw the small, flickering Fire. 'Feed me! Feed me!' cried Fire.

'What should I feed you?' Man asked. He had never seen Fire before.

'I eat sticks and logs,' Fire replied.

Man picked up a stick and gave it to Fire. Fire sent its flames flickering up the side of the stick until the stick started to burn. Man brought more and more sticks and Fire leapt and danced in delight. Man warmed himself by the blazing Fire, enjoying the colours of the flames and the hissing sound Fire made as it ate the wood. Man and Fire were very happy together and Man fed Fire sticks whenever it got hungry.

A long time later, Bear and his people came back to the edge of the forest, looking for Fire. Fire was angry when it saw Bear and it jumped and roared at him and drove him away. So from that day to this, Fire has belonged to Man.

S. E. Schlosser

Focus

1 What did Fire give Bear at the beginning of the story? Tick (✓) two things.

people ☐   cold ☐   warmth ☐   light ☐   darkness ☐

2 Where did Bear put Fire while he looked for food?

_____

3 Why didn't Bear come to feed Fire?

_____

4 a Who fed Fire when Bear didn't come?

_____

  b What did he feed Fire?

_____

  c How did he know what to give Fire to eat?

_____

5 Why did Fire drive Bear away?

_____

Practice

6 How did Fire feel when Bear first left him? Tick (✓) one adjective.

happy ☐   sad ☐   frightened ☐   lonely ☐

7 Why did Fire's feelings change after Bear had been gone a while?

_____

8 What do you think Man's first thoughts were on seeing Fire?

_____

9 When Fire decided to stay with Man how do you think Man felt? Why?

_____

_____

Challenge

10 Write two things you like about the story.

_____

_____

11 Write two things you might change about the story.

_____

_____

> 4.2 What is a myth?

Focus

1 Look again at *Bear and Fire*.

Circle the statements that suggest this story is a myth.

It doesn't have very many characters.

It explains why people have fire.

It is not a story that would happen in the real world.

It is an old story from Native Americans.

The characters are named after something from the natural world.

Practice

2 Write each of the fire words in the correct column to
   show which kind of word each one is.

   Some of the words will fit into more than one column.

Nouns	Verbs	Adjectives

3 Choose one noun, one verb and one adjective from the boxes.

   Write one sentence containing all three of these words.

   _____

   _____

Challenge

4 Ask your family and friends about myths from where you live.

   Write your favourite myth and share it with others.

   _____

   _____

_____

_____

_____

_____

_____

_____

_____

> 4.3 Looking at pronouns

Language focus

Pronouns can be used instead of nouns or noun phrases.

Examples:

nouns   Bear Fire forest stick

noun phrases   Bear and his people,   small flickering fire

pronouns   I he she it you him her they them

Bear is looking.   **He** is looking.

noun   pronoun

Using pronouns helps your writing flow.

Focus

1 Write each word in the correct column.

Nouns	Verbs	Pronouns

Practice

2 Read this paragraph and <u>underline</u> all the pronouns.
Then complete the table.

> Fire was worried. It had almost gone out. But Man heard its calls for help and he came. Fire told Man what it liked to eat and Man went to look for twigs and sticks. He placed them down beside Fire. While Fire devoured them, Man warmed himself.
>
> *S. E. Schlosser*

Nouns or noun phrase	Pronouns
Fire	
Man	
twigs and sticks	

Challenge

3 Complete the table of pronouns.

Male	he	him	himself
Female	she		
Plural		them	
Neither male nor female			itself

> 4.4 What is a legend?

Language focus

A **suffix** is usually a group of letters that is put at the end of a word to form a new word.

Example:

bright**est**   bright**ly**   bright**ness**

root word   suffix   root word   suffix   root word   suffix

–en, –ous, –ive, –ing, –er, –ed, –ful, –ion, –est, –ly, –ment, –less and –ness are all suffixes.

Some words have more than one suffix.

Example:

threat   threat**en**   threat**ened**

root word   root word   suffix   root word   suffix   suffix

Focus

1 <u>Underline</u> any words with a suffix in this paragraph from *Mulan*.

> At dawn she said goodbye to her family. She tied her hair up so she
> looked like a boy. Her family thought she would be back by the evening,
> but they were wrong. Three days later Mulan arrived at the army camp.
> She was nervous that the guard would notice she was a girl so she used
> her deepest voice. Mulan found army life hard. The days and nights were
> long and exhausting. She missed her family, but she didn't give up. She
> worked very hard to train for battle.
>
> Traditional, retold

Practice

2 Write the root word for each of these words.

Example: coming = come

a quietly = _____

b looked = _____

c suddenly = _____

d deepest = _____

e exhausting = _____

f impressed = _____

Reading tip

Knowing the root word of a suffixed word can help you with the meaning of a word.

Challenge

3 Without looking at a dictionary, write what you think each of these suffixed words mean.

a dangerous _____

b nervous _____

c beautiful _____

d deepest _____

e quietly _____

f impressed _____

> 4.5 Looking at paragraphs

Language focus

A **paragraph** is a section of text. Each paragraph is a group of sentences about one idea or event. Each paragraph starts on a new line and is sometimes indented.

Example:

In the beginning, Bear owned Fire. Fire warmed Bear and his people on cold days and it gave them light when the nights were long and dark. Bear always carried Fire with him.

    One day, Bear and his people went to a forest. Bear put Fire down at the edge of the forest, then Bear and his people went deeper and deeper into the forest to look for food ....

Focus

1 These words and phrases can be used to begin paragraphs.

Sort them into three groups: *When? Where?* and *When and Where?*

Write them in the diagram on the next page.

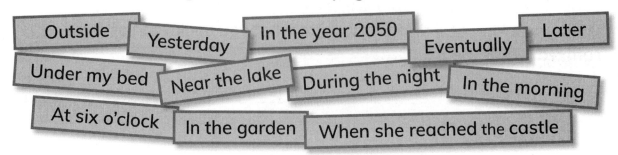

Outside   Yesterday   In the year 2050   Eventually   Later

Under my bed   Near the lake   During the night   In the morning

At six o'clock   In the garden   When she reached the castle

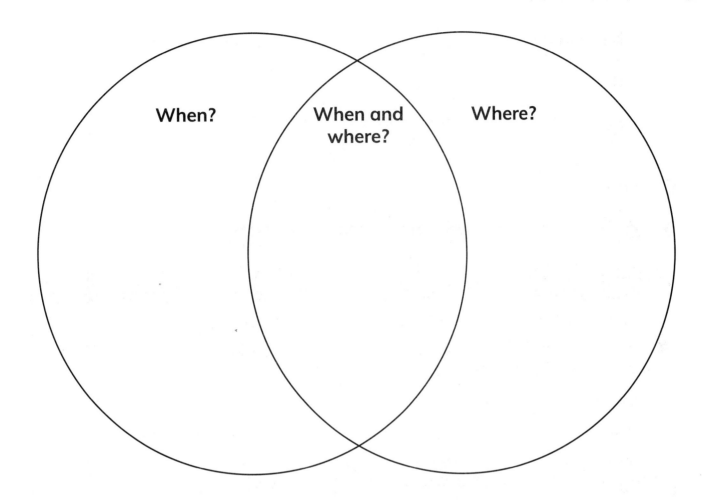

When?

When and where?

Where?

Practice

2 Complete the sentences with a suitable word or phrase from **Focus**.

a _____ the chief called a meeting and explained that the dragon was eating too many people.

b _____ they decided to ask if anyone would fight the dragon.

c _____ the girl said that she would like to try. Everyone laughed.

d _____ the girl set off to find the dragon.

e _____ she saw the

   dragon's cave.

f _____ there was an

   enormous dragon.

Challenge

3 Plan what you would write in three paragraphs about an interest you have.

   Write notes on what you will write about in each paragraph. For example:

Interest: Cricket

Paragraph 1:   Introduction to the game of cricket, how many
                   on a team, the main positions

Paragraph 2:   Why I enjoy cricket, how long I have played,
                   who taught me the game

Paragraph 3:   Information on the team I support, why I support
                   them, how well they do in the league

Interest: _____

Paragraph 1: _____

_____

_____

Paragraph 2: _____

_____

_____

Paragraph 3: _____

_____

_____

> 4.6 Joining sentences

Language focus

A **simple sentence** has only one action verb or verb phrase.

A simple sentence has one clause.

Example: Mulan's family did not **agree**.

Simple sentences can be joined together using **connectives** to make **multi-clause sentences**.

A multi-clause sentence has more than one clause:

Example:

She tied up her hair **so** she looked like a boy.

clause   connective   clause

Connectives can reflect time, place or cause.

Examples:

time connectives	=	first	next	last	then
place connectives	=	up	over	behind	
cause connectives	=	so	if	because	

Focus

1 <u>Underline</u> the clause or clauses in each of these sentences.

   a Jamilla had to find her watch so she could find out if she was late.

   b The cricket captain was nervous but he was sure they were going to win.

   c The snow covered everything overnight.

   d Kyle was hungry but he had
      no time to eat his lunch.

Remember, you can use a pronoun instead of repeating a noun or noun phrase if it is obvious who did the action.

Practice

2 Finish these multi-clause
   sentences using your own ideas.

   a The girl saw the enormous dragon _____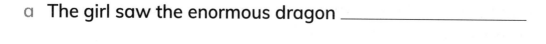

      _____

   b The dragon yawned _____

      _____

   c The dragon tried to make a flame _____

      _____

   d The girl said, 'Do you want to fight _____

      _____ ?'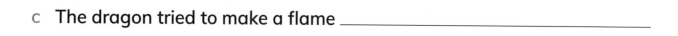

   e The dragon tried to fly away _____

      _____

f   The girl lifted her spear _____

_____

g   The dragon burst into tears _____

_____

Challenge

3   Write three of your own multi-clause sentences, each using
a different connective.

a   _____

_____

b   _____

_____

c   _____

_____

> 4.7 Making links

Focus

indigenous Australian: earliest known people to live in Australia

1 Read this indigenous Australian story.

A Visit From Strangers From Another Place

In the long ago past, there was a tribe of people who lived far, far away. They built their camp near a burning fire that never went out so that they could light their fire-sticks from it. They were the only people anywhere who had the use of fire.

One day, two brothers from the camp got bored and decided to go on a hunting trip to explore the world. 'We will go and hunt possum,' they agreed, 'and bring back enough for everybody.' So Kanbi and Jitabidi went out into the world and brought their fire-sticks with them. They left the sticks by a rock while they went hunting.

At first the fire-sticks were happy to lie and breathe in this strange new land. After a while, however, they became bored and started to play. They ran from place to place, and everywhere they ran the dry grass caught alight.

The fire grew and spread and roared and sent out black clouds of smoke. Kanbi and Jitabidi heard the flames and smelled the smoke and hurried back to put out the fire and collect their fire-sticks. However, the indigenous Australian people who lived in that part of the world had also heard the flames and smelled the smoke. They came to see what was happening. They had never seen fire before so they were frightened of this loud, orange monster. As the fire came closer, they felt its heat and they bathed in its light.

Before Kanbi and Jitabidi could finish putting out the fires, some of the indigenous Australian people had lit their own fire-sticks and were carrying them back to their camps. 'We must watch over these fire-sticks carefully and keep them burning forever,' they said to one another.

Kanbi and Jitabidi quickly gathered up their playful fire-sticks and returned to their campsite. They were afraid the indigenous Australian people would punish them for the damage they had caused. But the people were excited and grateful for the wonderful gift of fire.

a   Is this story a myth or a legend? _____

b   Explain your answer by giving two features of the genre that are in the story.

_____

_____

Practice

2   Complete the table.
Do your answers confirm if the story is a myth or a legend?

	A Visit From Strangers From Another Place
When?	
Where?	
Characters	
Main event	
Theme/ lesson	

Challenge

Answer these questions.

3 Read these statements about the strangers from another place. Tick (✓) two statements we know are true from the story.

   a They lived far, far away. ☐

   b They lived on the sun. ☐

   c They had fire. ☐

   d They liked possums. ☐

   e They wanted to give fire to the rest of the world. ☐

4 Why did Kanbi and Jitabidi come to where the indigenous Australian people lived?

_____

5 How did Kanbi and Jitabidi know that there was a fire?

_____

6 What did the indigenous Australian people think the fire was like?

_____

7 What made them like it better?

_____

8 In the last paragraph it says, 'They were afraid the indigenous Australian people would punish them ...'. Who are 'they'?

_____

9 Which word in paragraph 2 is used instead of said?

_____

> 4.8 Rewriting a myth

Focus

1 Working out the pattern of a known story lets you plan a new story based on the same pattern.

Look at the table. It shows a story pattern based on the stages of the story. Try to work out how the pattern is made. Then add the missing information.

Bear and Fire	Pattern
Bear owned Fire.	introducing characters 1 and 2
Bear left Fire by the edge of the wood and wandered off. Fire got hungry.	character 1 leaves character 2 character 2 needs character 1
Man came and fed Fire. Man and Fire became friends.	_____ characters 2 and 3 become friends
Bear came back. _____ Fire now belonged to Man.	character 1 returns character 2 chases character 1 away _____

Practice

2   Making a plan like the one in **Focus** is called 'boxing up' a story.

Try boxing up your own *Bear and Fire* myth.

Pattern	New story
introducing characters 1 and 2	
character 1 leaves character 2 character 2 needs character 1	
character 3 helps character 2 characters 2 and 3 become friends	
character 1 returns character 2 chases character 1 away characters 2 and 3 stay friends	

Challenge

3   Think of a story you know well. It doesn't have to be a myth.
    It might be a fairy tale, for example. Fill in both columns.
    What pattern does this story have?

New story	Pattern

> 4.9 Exploring a legend

> **Language focus**
>
> Some words use an **apostrophe** to show where a letter, or letters, have been missed out.
>
> **Example:**
>
> do **not** = don't   I **will** = I'll
>
> These words are called **contractions**.
>
> The apostrophe takes the place of the missing letter or letters.

Focus

1   Draw a line to match these words with their contractions.

Practice

2   Write the two words that make up each contraction.

a   he'll   =   _____   _____

b   should've =   _____   _____

c   isn't   =   _____   _____

d   that's   =   _____   _____

e   I'm   =   _____   _____

Challenge

3 Use each of these contractions in a sentence.

a don't _____

b I'll _____

c you're _____

d might've _____

e she's _____

> 4.10 Planning a legend

Focus

1 Plan a story about Sinbad.

Draw pictures showing what will happen in each paragraph in your story.

Paragraph 1	Paragraph 2

Paragraph 3

Paragraph 4

Paragraph 5

Paragraph 6

Practice

2   List the characters you are going to include in your story.

Describe each character.

Write their role in your story.

Character	Description	Role in story
Sinbad		

Challenge

3   Write adverbs or adverbial phrases you might include at the beginning of each paragraph.

Paragraph 1	
Paragraph 2	
Paragraph 3	
Paragraph 4	
Paragraph 5	
Paragraph 6	

> 4.11 Writing a legend

Language focus

Dialogue is another term for speech in stories. When you write dialogue you:

- start a new speaker on a new line
- use speech marks around the words characters say.

Speech marks like this " show where the words a character says **begin**.

Speech marks like this " show where the words a character says **end**.

Sometimes, speech marks are shown like this: '...'

Phrases like he said are not included inside the speech marks.

Example: "Use speech marks like this," he said.

Remember, there are lots of different words you can use instead of said like asked, replied, shouted, muttered.

Focus

1 All these verbs can be used instead of *said* but they don't all mean the same thing!

Complete the table to show how they are different.

How the words are said	Verbs
quietly	
in a questioning way	asked
loudly	
very loudly	
sadly	

Practice

2   Complete these past tense speech verbs.

a   shout   →   _____   f   cry   →   _____

b   query   →   _____   g   laugh   →   _____

c   smile   →   _____   h   ask   →   _____

d   reply   →   _____   i   notice   →   _____

e   enquire   →   _____   j   add   →   _____

Challenge

3 Copy these sentences. Add the missing speech marks and a different speech verb to each sentence.

a It is time we left, _____ Hussain.

_____

b We better hurry or we will be late, _____ Jacob.

_____

c Tom _____ Has the film started?

_____

d That was a brilliant story, _____ Leah.

_____

e Meena _____ I want to go and watch it again!

_____

> 4.12 Improving your legend

Language focus

Punctuation marks are used to help the reader make sense of the text. Learn and remember these.

. ! ?	Full stops, exclamation marks and question marks show the end of sentences.
,	Commas separate items in lists and ideas in sentences.
' '	Speech marks show the beginning and end of speech.

Focus

1 Fill in the missing punctuation.

a ___ I have been listening to the traders,' said the queen.

b 'What have you found out ___ ' asked her advisers ___

c 'They say that this new king is very wise, ___ replied the queen.

d 'Have you heard the stories ___ The man is already a legend ___

e I want to find out how wise he really is ___

Practice

2 Write sentences that include the following:

a a question mark and two commas

_____

b an exclamation mark and speech marks

_____

c a full stop, a comma and speech marks

_____

Challenge

3 Neatly copy a paragraph from your legend.

_____

_____

_____

_____

_____

_____

_____

_____

4 Now tick (✓) the statements that are true of your handwriting.

- It is easy to read. ☐

- The tall letters and the letters that go below the line ☐
  are a different height from the other letters.

- All the other letters are the same size. ☐

- The spaces between the letters in a word are about the same size. ☐

- The spaces between the words are about the same size. ☐

- All of my writing is joined. ☐

- Some of my writing is joined. ☐

- None of my writing is joined. ☐

5 Write your own handwriting target.

_____

_____

5 > Writing to each other

> 5.1 What do we write?

Focus

1 What sort of mail comes to your house in a week?
   Complete the table each day.

> You might get letters, postcards, parcels, advertisements or newspapers.

Day	What kind of mail?
Monday	
Tuesday	
Wednesday	
Thursday	
Friday	
Saturday	
Sunday	

Practice

Answer these questions.

2 Are there any days in the week when you didn't get post?

_____

3 Why don't you get post on some days?

_____

4 Is your post delivered or do you have to collect it?

_____

Challenge

5 Imagine you are writing a postcard to a cousin who lives abroad.

a Explain how the postcard will get from your house to his or hers.

b What do you need to include to make this happen?

_____

_____

6   Draw a stamp from where you live.

> 5.2 Scanning or reading carefully?

Language focus

Prepositions are words that show the relationship between a noun (or pronoun) with another word in the sentence. They often can show the 'position' of something.

Examples: My mother, who lives **in** England, is very ill.
              I will stay **with** my sister and her family.
              I will write to you **from** England.

Focus

1   <u>Underline</u> the preposition in each of these sentences.

  a   The cat ran through the bush.

  b   A bus stopped at the traffic lights.

  c   The children ran down the hill.

  d   We enjoy going to the shop.

  e   I slipped in the mud.

  f   Samra hid behind the curtain.

Practice

2 Write an 'opposite' preposition for each of the prepositions below.

a over _____

b in _____

c near _____

d below _____

3 Write another pair of opposite prepositions.

_____   _____

Challenge

4 Choose three prepositions.

_____   _____   _____

5 Write each preposition in a sentence.

a _____

b _____

c _____

6 Underline the preposition in each sentence you wrote.

> 5.3 Looking at synonyms

Language focus

Synonyms are words that have similar meanings.

Examples: cheerful is a synonym of happy.

miserable is a synonym of sad.

Using synonyms for ordinary words can make your writing more interesting and precise.

Focus

1   Draw lines to match the words that can be synonyms.

big	tiny
little	strange
good	horrid
sad	massive
nasty	miserable
odd	brilliant

Practice

2   Write sentences using the synonyms.

a   big   We saw a massive ship.

b   little   _____

c   good   _____

d   sad   _____

e   nasty   _____

f   odd   _____

Challenge

3 Write a synonym for these everyday verbs.

a make _____   e walk _____

b like _____   f want _____

c do _____   g see _____

d say _____

> # 5.4 What does a letter look like?

Language focus

When you write a letter you need to include five things:

1 **heading** – include the address of the person who is writing the letter and the date

2 **greeting** – who the letter is to

3 **body** – the information in the letter

4 **ending** – shows the letter has ended

5 **signature** – the name of the person who wrote the letter

Focus

1 Use the labels in the boxes to label the features of the letter.

28 Riverview Road,
Reading,
Berkshire,
RG9 5SN,
United Kingdom.
Saturday 17 May

Dear Class 3,

Yesterday, my sister looked after my mother for the day, so Arturo and I went for a day out in London. We had a very enjoyable time.

First we went to see Buckingham Palace, where Queen Elizabeth lives. It's a huge house. Arturo and I counted 68 windows! Why do you imagine the Queen and her husband need that many rooms?

After leaving the palace, we strolled in the sun beside the River Thames. It's a very wide river and it's extremely busy with ships, speedboats, water taxis and water buses. There are even river police!

Then we went to Westminster and saw the Houses of Parliament. This is where the government makes the laws in the UK. The Houses of Parliament are next to the Thames.

Finally we went across Westminster Bridge for a ride on the London Eye. This was Arturo's favourite part of the day! The London Eye is a massive wheel. You've probably seen it on TV because they set off fireworks from the London Eye for important celebrations. You can see some excellent views of London from the top.

I hope you are working hard and learning lots of things. I miss you all.

From,

Mrs Sabell

Practice

2 Write the heading you would use if you were writing a letter.

_____

_____

_____

_____

_____

Challenge

3 How would you sign your name if you wrote a letter to:

a friend? _____

b your teacher? _____

c someone who didn't know you? _____

› 5.5 Looking at homophones

Language focus

A **homophone** is a word that sounds the same as another word but has a different meaning and spelling.

Examples:

dear deer here hear write right

Focus

1 Match the homophone pairs with a line.

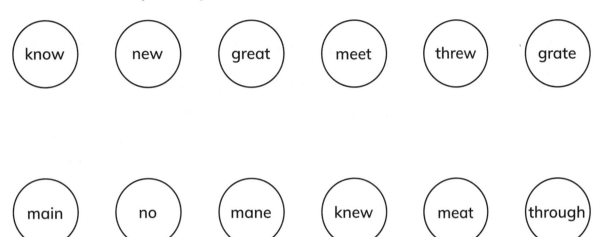

Practice

2 <u>Underline</u> all the homophones in these sentences.

    a It is time you went to the party.

    b Arturo is eight years old.

    c I would love a piece of his birthday cake.

    d Can I have a slice of cake too?

Challenge

3 For some homophones there are three words that sound the same but have different meanings and spellings.

Add two more homophones to these words.
Use a dictionary if you need help.

    a to   _____   _____

    b sow   _____   _____

    c they're   _____   _____

> 5.6 A letter of complaint

Focus

1 If you were to write a letter of complaint, what would you write about?

   • Write down three things you might complain about.

   • For each one, write who you would complain to.

Complaint	Who to complain to

Practice

2 Choose one of your ideas from **Focus** and plan a letter of complaint.
   Answer these questions.

   a Why are you writing?

   _____

   _____

   b What evidence do you have for the complaint?

   _____

   _____

c How has the situation made you feel?

_____

_____

d What would you like to happen?

_____

_____

Challenge

3 Use the notes from Activities 1 and 2 to write the 'body' of the letter of complaint.

Remember to:

- write in a formal style
- use powerful words to get your point across
- write multi-clause sentences with connectives.

_____

_____

_____

_____

_____

_____

_____

› 5.7 Beginning and ending letters

Focus

1 Sort these types of letters into two sets in the table below: formal and informal.

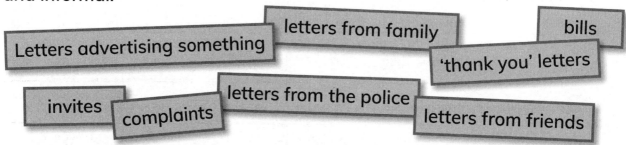

letters from family

bills

Letters advertising something

'thank you' letters

invites

letters from the police

complaints

letters from friends

Formal letters	Informal letters

Practice

2   Write a greeting for each type of letter.

Type of letter	Greeting
letters from the police	Dear Mr Franke
letters from family	
invites	
letters from friends	
bills	
complaints	
'thank you' letters	

Challenge

3   Write a letter ending for each type of letter.

Type of letter	Letter ending
letters from the police	Yours sincerely
letters from family	
invites	
letters from friends	
bills	
complaints	
'thank you' letters	

> 5.8 Looking at sentences in a letter

Flat 35,
Triveni Apartments,
Pitampur Road,
Kochi,
Kerala 682024,
India.

Dear Mummy and Daddy,

We're having a good time with Grandmother.

We have just come back from a trip to the beach. It seemed to take a long time to get there and the beach was quite crowded. At first I thought that the trip was going to be a waste of time, but I soon changed my mind.

First Grandmother gave us money for a drink and we both felt better after that. Then she found an empty piece of beach and put up a sort of beach tent. It was great! We could change in private, and so we were soon splashing around in the water. When we came out, it was good to have the tent to get out of the sun. Can we get a tent like that?

I hope you are having a quiet time without us.

Lots of love,

Padma

Focus

1 Scan the text and answer these questions.

a Who is Padma staying with? _____

b Where did they go? _____

c What did they use the tent for? _____

Practice

2 Read slowly and carefully to find the answers to these questions.

a Is Padma staying with Grandmother by herself?

_____

b How did Padma feel when she first got to the beach?

_____

c Why did she get changed?

_____

d Do you think Padma is missing her Mummy and Daddy? Why?

_____

Challenge

3 Copy sentences from the letter. Write:

a a question   _____

b a statement   _____

c an exclamation _____

4 Write your own examples of sentences that Padma might add to her letter.

a a question   Please can we come back to see grandmother soon?

b a statement   _____

c an exclamation _____

> 5.9 Other written communication

Focus

Read the SMS message Mrs Sabella wrote to Class 3 at the airport.

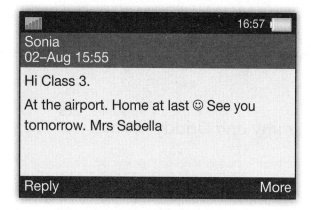

1 Write an SMS message on the phone in response. Remember, you don't have to write using sentences!

Practice

2 Rewrite these SMS messages using sentences with a verb or a verb phrase.

a At cricket yesterday?

_____

b Happy at your news.

_____

c With Juanita at playtime.

_____

d Tea?

_____

e Good day at school?

_____

Challenge

3 a Read this email and (circle) all the pronouns you can find.

Date: 4 August 21:15

From: Sonia.sabell@lemail.com

To: Arturo.Bilardo@email.co.uk

Subject: Missing you already

Dear Arturo,

I have been home for only three hours but I have been very busy! I had to collect my cats from Mrs Menotti. She looked after them while I was with you. She is very kind, but she wanted me to sit down and tell her all about you.

The plane I flew home in was very big. It had over 300 seats but they were very close together. Near me was a family. The three children didn't like sitting down for so long and kept running around. Looking at them made me think of you but I think you would have sat more quietly than they did.

I need to go to bed now. I have to go to school tomorrow and meet all the lovely children in Class 3. I wonder if they have missed me?

With very much love,

Aunty Sonia

b Complete the table to show which pronouns are used instead of the nouns or noun phrases.

Noun or noun phrase	Pronouns
Aunty Sonia Arturo	I, me, my
Mrs Menotti	
cats plane seats	
children on the plane children in Class 3	

> 5.10 Talking about mail

Read the two texts.

ARGENTINA LUXURY TOUR

An unforgettable experience
22-day holiday
All for just £1195!!

Argentina holiday highlights:

- Visit Buenos Aires, city of culture.
- Go to a milonga and learn to dance the tango.
- Taste fantastic food.
- See the mighty Iguazu Falls.
- Explore the hot, humid Argentine rainforest.

Argentinian Holidays
56 Baker Street
London
NW1 6XE

Dear Mrs Evans,

Do you need a holiday?

Do you need a rest or are you looking for adventure?

Come to Argentina for your holiday of a lifetime!

Argentina is one of the world's largest countries. It is made for your perfect holiday!

Relax on a cruise off the Antarctic shores. Why not go whale-watching or swimming in the warm Southern Atlantic Ocean?

Or have an adventure herding cattle as a gaucho in the Pampas grasslands!

If you like excitement, how about climbing in the Andes?

Or if cities are more your thing, just head for the vibrant city of Buenos Aires.

Other experiences not to be missed:

- Go to a football match at Boca Juniors or River Plate stadium.
- Drink a delicious cup of mate.
- Learn to tango.
- Swim in the South Atlantic Ocean from one of the beautiful beach resorts.

So what are you waiting for, Mrs Evans? Please come and join us in sunny Argentina!

Yours sincerely,
Linda Matthews
Customer Travel Advisor
0044 1234 567890 or info@holidays_in_argentina.co.uk

Focus

1 Tick (✓) the statements that are true.

 a The letter is from Linda Matthews. ☐

 b The letter is from Mrs Evans. ☐

 c Linda is a friend of Mrs Evans. ☐

 d Linda is giving Mrs Evans information about her family. ☐

 e Linda wants Mrs Evans to go on holiday to Argentina. ☐

 f The purpose of the letter is to report news of events in Argentina. ☐

 g The purpose of the letter is to make Mrs Evans want to visit Argentina. ☐

 h The letter is fiction. ☐

 i The letter is non-fiction. ☐

Practice

2 Find these sentences in the texts. What do the underlined words mean? You can use a dictionary to help.

 a Go to a milonga and learn to dance the tango.

   Milonga means _____.

 b See the mighty Iguazu Falls.

   Mighty means _____.

 c Explore the hot, humid Argentine rainforest.

   Humid means _____.

d Relax on a <u>cruise</u> off the Antarctic shores.

Cruise means _____ .

e Have an adventure herding cattle as a <u>gaucho</u>.

Gaucho means _____ .

Challenge

3 Write your own letter that advertises a place you would like to visit.

> 5.11 Writing a letter

Look at this first draft of Arturo's letter to his Aunty Sonia.

---

28 Riverview Road,
Reading,
Berkshire,
RG9 5SN,
United Kingdom.
Sunday 18 May

Dear Aunty Sonia,

Thank you for takeing me out to London. I had a nice time. I liked it when we went on the big train. The train was big. It was shiny. It was green. I liked it when the train went through the tunnel. It made my eyes feel strange when we came out of the tunnel into the lite.

The cat is watching TV with me. Her kittens are playing. they are making a sound. It is a big sound. They are going around the room. The cat is purring.

Lots of love,

Arturo

Focus

1 Cross out three common words on the letter.
Replace them with more powerful synonyms.

Practice

2 Make three multi-clause sentences in the letter by adding connectives.

Challenge

3   Rewrite the letter.

   a   Include your three powerful synonyms.

   b   Include your three multi-clause sentences.

   c   Correct three mistakes.

_____

_____

_____

_____

_____

_____

_____

_____

_____

_____

_____

_____

> 5.12 Improving your letter

Language focus

Punctuation is important in your writing.

- Use a **capital letter** at the beginning of your sentences and for people's names and place names.
- End every sentence with a **full stop** (.), a **question mark** (?) or an **exclamation mark** (!).
- Use **commas** (,) to separate items in lists.
- Use an **apostrophe** (') to show where you have joined two words together and shortened them.

Focus

1 Add the missing punctuation to this letter.
Write any missing capital letters.

Dear arturo,

I cant believe that its been a week since I last saw you so much has happened in the week

I was so pleased to get back to school and meet Class 3 again I knew it would be exciting to hear about their lessons with the other teacher I asked them to write about what they had been doing since I last saw them they have been very busy

what have you been doing I wish I didn't live so far away it would be so good to see you more often love from aunty sonia

Remember, an apostrophe shows where two words have been joined together and then shortened:
you are → you're
they will → they'll.

Practice

2 Complete the tables to show the words in full and the shortened forms with an apostrophe.

Words in full	Shortened form
is not	isn't
	can't
would not	
was not	
	couldn't
	aren't
were not	
will not	

Words in full	Shortened form
I am	I'm
	he's
it is	
we are	
	they're
I will	
	you'll
	we'll

Challenge

3 Complete the spelling log for five words you want to learn to spell.

Word	Tricky bit	Other words with the same spelling pattern		
learn	ear	earn	early	earth

6 ▶ Bringing stories alive

> 6.1 Reading a playscript

Four Clever Brothers, **Part 1**

Characters

Judge – the narrator and wise man

Gilad – a foolish man

The four brothers:

Tazim – the eldest brother, a natural leader, his brothers look up to him

Kamran – a hard worker

Sadiq – a serious young man

Latif – the youngest brother

Stage directions
Four brothers walking along a path between two villages. The path is dry and sandy, with grass growing on each side. As they walk, the brothers speak softly to each other. Judge is standing to the side of the stage.

Judge: I am Adil the judge. I am going to tell you a story. It takes place in a dry and dusty desert land.

My story concerns Gilad, the camel owner, who came to me one hot afternoon to settle an argument. This was an unusual case, and I remember it well. Everything I will tell you is true.

There once were four brothers, who were very good hunters. Their father taught them how to track an animal by listening and looking for clues on the ground.

Tazim: Do you see footprints on this path? Look, just here.

Kamran: It looks like something has passed this way recently.

Sadiq: They are smaller than the prints of a horse's hoof.

Latif: But they are spaced well apart. I would say it was a camel.

Tazim: Yes, that's just what I was thinking.

Suddenly, a man rushes towards the four brothers, waving his arms in distress.

Gilad: Help! You, there! Please help me. Have you seen my camel? I'm sure someone has stolen it!

Judge: The four brothers looked at each other with worried faces. Then they looked at the camel owner.

Lynne Rickards

Focus

1 Read the beginning of this play. Write which character said each of the following.

  a I am going to tell you a story. _____

  b Do you see footprints on this path? _____

  c I would say it was a camel. _____

  d Please help me. _____

  e Then they looked at the camel owner. _____

Practice

2 Answer these questions.

a What is the Judge's name?

_____

_____

b Who did Tazim agree with?

_____

_____

c Who came rushing towards the brothers?

_____

_____

d How do we know Gilad is a foolish man?

_____

_____

e Do you think someone has stolen the camel?

_____

_____

Challenge

3 Write what you think happens next in the play.

_____

_____

_____

_____

_____

_____

Session 6.2 tells you what happens next in the play.
See if you were correct!

> 6.2 Looking closely at a playscript

Language focus

A **playscript** needs:

- a title
- a list of characters
- stage directions
- dialogue.

Focus

1 Add the correct labels from the boxes to the playscript.

Four Clever Brothers, **Part 1**

a _____

b _____

Judge – the narrator and wise man

Gilad – a foolish man

The four brothers:

Tazim – the eldest brother, a natural leader, his brothers look up to him

Kamran – a hard worker

Sadiq – a serious young man

Latif – the youngest brother

c _____

Stage directions

Four brothers walking along a path between two villages. The path is dry and sandy, with grass growing on each side. As they walk, the brothers speak softly to each other. Judge is standing to the side of the stage.

d _____

Judge: I am Adil the judge. I am going to tell you a story. It takes place in a dry and dusty desert land.

Lynne Rickards

Practice

2 Write a sentence for each playscript feature explaining
why it is important.

a Title _____

_____

b Character list _____

_____

c Stage directions _____

_____

d Dialogue _____

_____

Challenge

3 Read through this part of the playscript.
It has one stage direction shown in *italic*.

Add three more stage directions.

> ***Four Clever Brothers*, Part 2**
>
> **Tazim:**   We would like to help you, sir.
>   Tell me, is your camel blind in one eye?
>
> **Gilad:**   Yes, it is!
>
> **Kamran:** And is it lame in one foot?

Gilad:	Yes, that is true too! It is an old camel, and a bad-tempered beast, but it's the only one I've got.
Sadiq:	I'm sure we can help you find it.
Latif:	Tracking animals is what we do best.
Gilad:	(*to himself*) I am very pleased that the brothers seem to know my camel so well. But I wonder how that is possible.
Sadiq:	I have another question for you, sir. Was your camel carrying a sack of wheat on one side?
Gilad:	Indeed it was.
Latif:	And did it have a jar of honey on the other side?
Gilad:	That is exactly right! Come, come, you must think I am a fool. How do you know so much about my camel? You four men must have stolen my camel?

Lynne Rickards

> 6.3 Writing dialogue and performing a play

Focus

1 Draw a cartoon strip in the four boxes on the next page, showing something that happened to you.

> Did you visit somewhere exciting? Did something funny happen to you?

2 Add two speech bubbles to each box.

Practice

3 Write the information from your cartoon as if it were a story.

Remember to start a new line when a new person speaks and include interesting verbs that describe the dialogue.

_____

_____

_____

_____

_____

_____

_____

_____

_____

_____

_____

_____

Challenge

4 Finally, write the same information from your cartoon as if it were a playscript.

Title: _____

Characters: _____

_____

_____

Stage directions: _____

_____

_____

_____

Character	Dialogue
_____	_____
_____	_____
_____	_____
_____	_____
_____	_____
_____	_____
_____	_____
_____	_____

> 6.4 What happens next?

Language focus

Often the c in a word sounds like a c. This is called a *hard* c.

Sometimes the c in a word can sound like an s. This is called a *soft* c.

Example: **Latif:** Believe us, sir. We have never even seen your camel. We are innocent!

camel = c as in cat (hard c)

innocent = c as in nice (soft c)

Focus

1 Circle all the words with a soft c.

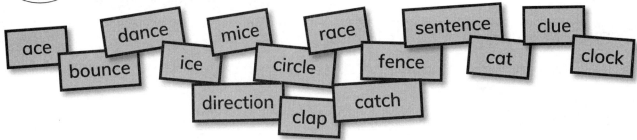

ace   dance   mice   race   sentence   clue
bounce   ice   circle   fence   cat   clock
direction   clap   catch

Practice

2 Write as many words as you can ending in –ice.

3 Write as many words as you can ending in –ace.

Challenge

4 Write a sentence that uses as many soft c words as you can.
<u>Underline</u> all the soft c words.

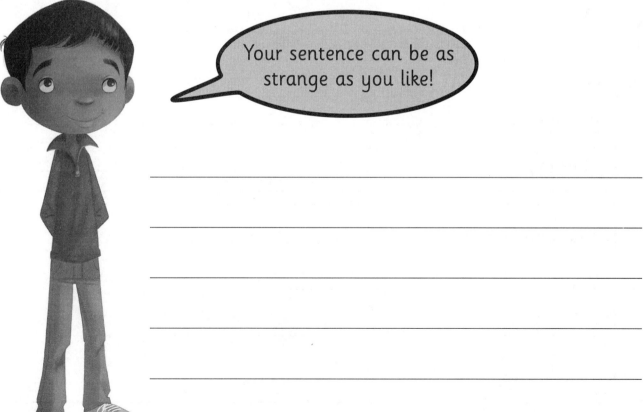

Your sentence can be as
strange as you like!

> 6.5 Writing a playscript

Use this information to plan a play:

- a poor, elderly woman or man sitting against a wall
- children walking towards her or him.

Focus

1 Fill in these character profiles:

Character name: _____

Age: _____

Appearance: _____

Role in play: _____

Character name: _____

Age: _____

Appearance: _____

Role in play: _____

Character name: _____

Age: _____

Appearance: _____

Role in play: _____

Practice

2   Describe the play setting.

_____

_____

_____

_____

_____

_____

Challenge

3   Fill in this story board.

Draw pictures and write notes. Include possible stage directions.

_____ _____ _____	_____ _____ _____

```



_____        _____


_____        _____


_____        _____
```

> 6.6 Improving a playscript

Read the playscript.

Four Clever Brothers, Part 3

Judge: So Gilad had the four brothers arrested and brought to me

Gilad: Adil, you are a man of justice. Here my plea! These for men have stolen my camel and they must be punished. Will you help me

Judge: Very well, Gilad. I will question them. Wat do you four men have to say for yourselves? How do you no so much about the missing camel

Tazim: It is very simpel, sir I could tell the camel was blind in one eye because the grass was eaten only on one side of the path. Clearly, the camel did not see the grass on the other side.

Gilad:	Humph. That is nonsense How can he tell anythin from a bit of grass
Judge:	Be patient, Gilad. We must hear all they have to say before making a judgement. Leve this to me

Lynne Rickards

Focus

1 Add any missing punctuation to the playscript.

Practice

2 <u>Underline</u> any words that are incorrectly spelled. Write the correct spelling above.

3 Circle any homophones spelled incorrectly. Write the correct spelling above.

Challenge

4 Add three noun phrases to the playscript.

5 Circle three words or phrases and write a synonym above.

7 ▶ Going on an adventure

› 7.1 Reading an adventure

Focus

1 Look at the photographs. Which of these adventures would you most like to have? Choose one and write a short paragraph to explain why you would like to have this adventure.

_____

_____

_____

_____

_____

Practice

2 Add punctuation to this passage. You can use full stops, capital letters, question marks, exclamation marks, commas and apostrophes.

> Fernando hurried after his brother and sister he didnt want to go but he knew they would never forgive him if he didnt he felt in the pockets of his shorts to see what he could find he found a piece of string three coins and his catapult he pulled out his catapult now he felt better he hurried on after his brother and sister

Challenge

3 Read the passage in **Practice** again.

List eight words you might use to describe Fernando.
One has been done for you.

concerned _____ _____ _____

_____ _____ _____ _____

› 7.2 Story beginnings

Focus

1 Tick (✓) the story beginnings that might be from adventure stories.

a

> The night was dark and the wind howled. Alone on the vast ocean a tiny boat bobbed up and down. Inside the boat, a small child lay sobbing.
>
> Suddenly, the child raised her head and screamed a single word: 'Daddy!'

b

Tony the tiger walked to the flower shop.

'Hello,' he said to Rupert the rhino. Rupert lived in the house next door to Tony's and owned the flower shop. Rupert was always happy in his shop.

c

'Why can't I be in the team?' sobbed Vincent. 'I'm *nearly* eight. My birthday is in two months' time.'

'Don't cry, Vincent,' said his mother. 'It won't do you any good. Keep practising so that when you *are* eight you'll be good enough to join the team. Now come on, dry your eyes and let's go the market – we'll choose a nice fish for our dinner.'

d

'Shhh!' whispered Petra. 'You'll wake everyone up!'

Kaspar didn't say anything. He just hobbled after his sister's bobbing torchlight. His bag was heavy on his shoulder. He hadn't known how long they would be away so he had packed most of his belongings, just in case. They were going to find their uncle, but Kaspar wasn't sure why. Suddenly he felt frightened. He made a grab for his sister's hand but only got a handful of her dress. He kept tightly hold of it, feeling braver like that. Petra would keep him safe.

2 **Why do you think these stories might be adventure stories?**

_____

_____

_____

Practice

3 Complete the following with adjectives from the boxes.

beautiful deep fast golden long old
cracked everlasting frightened hidden lost
scary sweet twisted
ripe soft tall winding

a The _____ snake _____   ☐

b The tree is _____   ☐

c The roots are _____ and _____   ☐

d A _____ branch   ☐

e The sound was _____ and _____   ☐

f The _____ river   ☐

g The _____ pool   ☐

h The sand is _____ and _____   ☐

i Some _____ fruit   ☐

j The children are _____ and _____   ☐

Challenge

4 For the activity in **Practice**, decide whether you have made
   a noun phrase or a sentence.

   a Write **N** for a noun phrase, or **S** for a sentence, next to each one.

   b Add in the correct punctuation for any sentences.

5　What is the difference between a sentence and a noun phrase?

　　Write a sentence to explain.

_____

_____

_____

> ## 7.3　What happens next?

Language focus

Figurative language uses words and phrases to describe things.
It helps you to imagine what they look like.

When a writer describes something by saying it is like or as something
else, this is a type of figurative language called a **simile**.

Example:

> A dark cave opened up **like** a yawning mouth …
> between rocks **as sharp as** dragon fangs.

Focus

1　<u>Underline</u> the similes in this passage.

> So I climbed aboard and paddled away. The stream got bigger and the water
> flowed faster, and soon I was racing along as fast as a speedboat.
>
> I saw a huge boulder blocking the river. It was shaped like a dragon's head
> and my boat raced straight towards it. Help! I thought I was going to crash.
>
> Then, with an awful grinding noise, the rock began to move. A dark cave
> opened up like a yawning mouth, and I was swept inside.

Whoosh! I whizzed along a gloomy tunnel, holding on tight as my boat zigzagged between rocks as sharp as dragon fangs.

The water roared and my boat spun round and round. Soon I couldn't tell which way was home.

Suddenly, I shot out of the tunnel and found myself floating on a choppy sea. In the distance was a small island, with a plume of smoke billowing up from behind some trees. I steered my boat towards it.

Nick Ward

Practice

2 Write sentences that include these similes.

   a as black as the night

   _____

   _____

   b eat like a horse

   _____

   _____

   c as free as a bird

   _____

   _____

   d sleep like a log

   _____

   _____

Challenge

3 Write a simile about each of these subjects.

water _____

clouds _____

4 Write two more similes of your own.

Simile 1: _____

Simile 2: _____

> 7.4 Character portraits

Focus

1 a Circle the words in the boxes you might use to describe the girl in the image.

curious thoughtful lazy selfish

helpful famous interested scared

brave unknown

boring musical imaginative adventurous

b Add four more words you might use to describe her.

_____   _____

_____   _____

Practice

2 Choose six words from the boxes in **Focus** and use each of them to write sentences about the girl.

My six words are: _____ _____ _____

_____ _____ _____

_____

_____

_____

_____

_____

_____

Challenge

3 Use your words and sentences from **Focus** and **Practice** to write a character portrait about the girl.

- What is her name?
- Where does she come from?
- What is she like?
- What is she thinking and feeling?

_____

_____

_____

_____

_____

_____

_____

_____

_____

_____

_____

〉 7.5 Looking at chapters

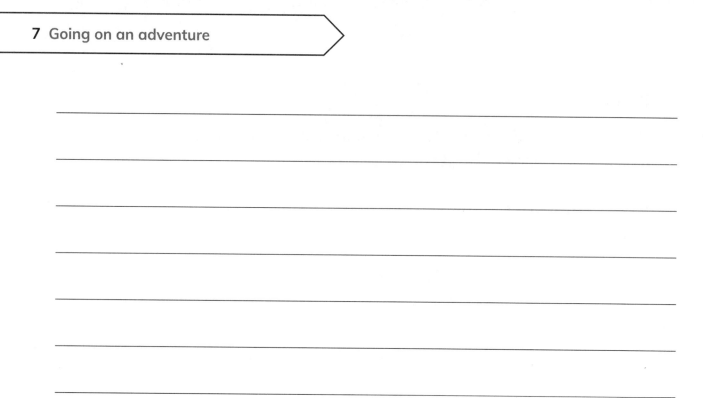

Language focus

Sentence openings can tell you:

- when something happens   **Example:** Later that day
- where something happens   **Example:** In the distance
- how something happens   **Example:** Slowly and carefully ...

Focus

1 Write these five chapter headings in the order you might use them in a story. Think carefully about what might happen in a story using these chapters.

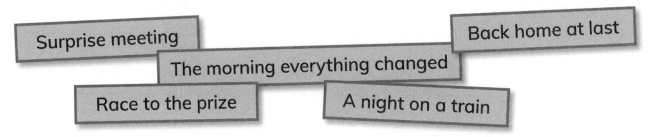

Surprise meeting

Back home at last

The morning everything changed

Race to the prize

A night on a train

Chapter 1: _____

Chapter 2: _____

Chapter 3: _____

Chapter 4: _____

Chapter 5: _____

Practice

2   Now write a sentence opening for each of the chapters in **Focus**.

Chapter 1: _____

Chapter 2: _____

Chapter 3: _____

Chapter 4: _____

Chapter 5: _____

Challenge

3   Complete this table with three different sentence openings about when, where or how something happens.

Sentence openings		
When	Where	How

> 7.6 Looking at verbs

Language focus

To make the past tense of most verbs you add –ed or –d.

Example: look<u>ed</u>   argu<u>ed</u>

But some verb forms don't follow this rule.
They are known as **irregular verbs**.

Example: sing → sang   go → went

Focus

1 Circle the correct verb to make sentences in the simple past tense.

   a I sleep / slept until my alarm went off.

   b We drink / drank five glasses of water in a day.

   c They caught / catch a train early in the morning.

2 Write the simple past tense verb in each of these sentences.

   a We _____ a cake for tea.

   b Nina _____ ten centimetres in a year.

   c I _____ six lengths of the pool.

Practice

The verb to be is an irregular verb.

3 Complete the table.

Present tense	Past tense
I am	I was
you are	
he is	

7.7 Looking in more detail

Present tense	Past tense
she is	she was
it is	
we are	we were
they are	

Challenge

4 Write the family verb for each of these irregular verbs.

a came   to _come_

b bought   to _____

c ate   to _____

d gave   to _____

e spoke   to _____

f made   to _____

g grew   to _____

h ran   to _____

⟩ 7.7 Looking in more detail

Read the passage.

Fire Snatcher

'You see, Lily, the villagers needed fire to warm their homes, and cook their food, and make life good. So they chose the biggest, bravest man in the village. They gave him a fine spear and they called him Fire Snatcher. My da, your great-granda, Lily, was Fire Snatcher and hero of the village.'

149 ⟩

'But how did he snatch the fire?' asked Lily.

'Well, Lily, dragons are strange creatures,' said Granda. 'They lay their eggs, then sleep for a full ninety years until the eggs are ready to hatch. When that happens, the dragon mothers wake up to care for their babies. The dragons were in their sleep-years when my da was Fire Snatcher. All he had to do was creep, tiptoe-quiet into the hills, then jump, suddenly, on a sleeping dragon and poke it with his spear. The poor beast would start from its sleep and blaze with fright, just as you or I would if anybody jabbed at us with a needle while we were sleeping. But it worked. It made the dragon roar fire. As it roared, the Fire Snatcher thrust his torch of dry wood into the flare of the dragon's fiery breath to light it.'

Pippa Goodhart

Focus

1 Underline any sentences about the Fire Snatcher.

Practice

2 Think about the Fire Snatcher as he goes to get the fire from the sleeping dragons.

Write three words or phrases to describe what you think the Fire Snatcher can:

a see or hear _____ _____ _____

b feel _____ _____ _____

Challenge

3 Imagine you are the Fire Snatcher. Write a description that describes when you discover the sleeping dragons. Use the words you wrote in **Practice** to help you describe what you see, hear and feel.

_____

_____

_____

_____

_____

_____

_____

> 7.8 Setting and dialogue

Language focus

Punctuate speech correctly.

- Use a new line for each speaker.
- Put opening speech marks (') at the beginning of the words that were said.
- Put closing speech marks (') at the end of the words that were said.
- If needed, put question marks (?) and exclamation marks (!) before the closing speech marks.
- Don't forget capital letters and full stops.

Focus

1 Add the missing speech marks to these sentences.

   a I am reading this book on dragons, said Rupesh.

   b It is a good book, replied Sam.

   c I love reading about dragons, Rupesh explained.

   d So do I, laughed Sam.

Practice

2 Copy the sentences. Add the missing punctuation and capital letters.

   a do you believe in dragons asked rupesh.

   _____

   b I'm not sure replied sam.

   _____

   c what about you queried sam.

   _____

   d definitely exclaimed rupesh.

   _____

Challenge

3 a Look at this conversation about Dragon Boy.
     Add the missing punctuation in the small boxes.

b In each of the gaps write a word that could replace *said*.
   Choose from these words.

answered   demanded   interrupted   replied   smiled
asked   exclaimed   laughed   responded   wondered

☐ Did Dragon Boy know that he was a human ☐ ☐ _____
Lily ☐

☐ No, ☐ _____ Granda. "He grew up with dragons ☐ They
were his brothers and sisters and his friends. ☐

☐ Could he do everything that they could do ☐ ☐ _____ Lily.

Granda _____ , ☐ No, he couldn't fly. But most of

all he couldn't make fire. That's what he wanted most. ☐

☐ What happened to him ☐ ☐ _____ Lily.

☐ You'll have to wait and find out later, ☐ _____ Granda ☐

> 7.9 More about paragraphs

Language focus

Writers usually begin a **new paragraph** when they introduce
a different action, a different time or a different place.

Interesting sentence openings at the beginning of each paragraph
lead the reader through the story.

Look at the picture story. Then do the activities.

Focus

1 Show how the story could be organised into six paragraphs.
Write what each paragraph will be about.

Paragraph	What the paragraph is about
1	
2	
3	
4	
5	
6	

Practice

2 Now write an opening sentence for each paragraph. Remember how
the opening sentences can lead the reader through the story.

Paragraph	Opening sentences
1	
2	
3	
4	
5	
6	

Challenge

3 Write the final paragraph for this story.
Use the opening sentence you wrote in **Practice**.

_____

_____

_____

_____

_____

_____

> 7.10 Looking at stories

Language focus

A **prefix** is a group of letters added before a word.

The prefix changes the meaning of the word and makes a new word.

Example: re– + view = <u>re</u>view

Each prefix adds a particular meaning to a root word.

Focus

1 Complete these word sums.

a dis + appear = _____

b un + fair = _____

Grammar tip

When prefixes are added to a root word, the root word doesn't change.

c re + appear   = _____

d mis + behave   = _____

e re + write   = _____

f dis + agree   = _____

g in + correct   = _____

h re + view   = _____

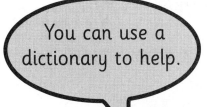

You can use a dictionary to help.

Practice

2 Write two words using each of these prefixes.

a un _____   _____

b re _____   _____

c dis _____   _____

d in _____   _____

Challenge

3 Look at the words you have written in **Practice**.

How has adding the prefix to the root word changed each word?

a The prefix *un*– means _____

b The prefix *re*– means _____

c The prefix *dis*– means _____

d The prefix *in*– means _____

> 7.11 Writing a story

Read the story.

One day Gopal was bored. He went into his garden. He found an egg. He picked it up. He took it home.

In bed later that night, Gopal looked at the egg. It was a big egg.

The next day the egg cracked. It was a dragon.

After a week the dragon made fire. It set the house on fire.

Sadly, the dragon flew away.

Focus

1 Do you think the story is well written? _____

2 Write what you could do to improve the story.

_____

_____

_____

_____

Practice

3 Write short character descriptions for Gopal and the dragon.

a Gopal _____

_____

b the dragon _____

_____

Challenge

4 Rewrite the story. Remember to include:

- paragraphs
- character descriptions
- powerful and interesting words
- interesting sentence openings

- a mixture of simple and multi-clause sentences and a range of connectives
- dialogue.

_____

_____

_____

_____

_____

_____

_____

_____

_____

_____

_____

_____

> 7.12 Improving your story

Focus

1 Copy these adjectives into the matching word group. Some adjectives may fit into more than one word group.

Scary words

Night-time words

Happy words

Practice

2 Write a noun phrase for each of these nouns.

a book _____

b river _____

c boat _____

d bird _____

e car _____

Challenge

3 Choose five words from your writing that were difficult to spell. Write them in the first column of the spelling log and complete the table.

Word	Tricky bit	Word	Similar word
found	ou	found	sound

8 > Wonderful world

> 8.1 Holidays

Focus

1   Where in the world do you live?
    Draw a cross on the map to show the country you live in.

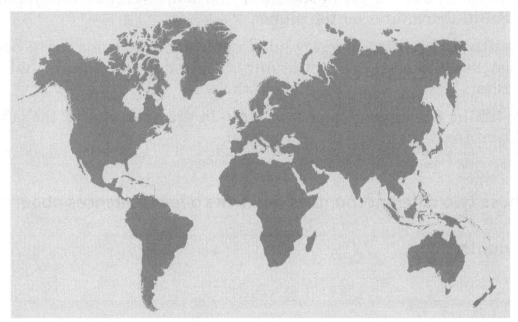

Practice

2   Complete this text about where you live and where you like to go on holiday.

The name of the city I live in or near is _____ and the

name of my country is _____ . People come here to see

_____ and _____ . When I go on holiday,

I like to go to _____ because it has _____ and

_____ . When I am on holiday I like to _____ and

_____ .

Challenge

3 Look at the information about Brazil and South Africa.
This is from a holiday fact file.

> **Brazil** has some great beaches and the city of Rio de Janeiro is famous for its carnival in the spring, when everyone dresses up and dances through the streets.
>
> Brazil is famous for the Amazon rainforest where visitors can see enormous trees, the Amazon River and some of the rarest and most beautiful creatures on the planet.
>
> **South Africa** attracts many holidaymakers, who come for its beautiful beaches and open areas of countryside, and for the safaris that allow visitors to see African animals in the wild.
>
> With the flat-topped Table Mountain in the background, the city of Cape Town is famous for its harbour.

4 Choose two different countries and write a few sentences about each one.

a **Country:**

_____

_____

_____

_____

_____

_____

_____

b **Country:**

_____

_____

_____

_____

_____

_____

_____

_____

> 8.2 In the library

Focus

1 Read these book titles. Do you think they are fiction or non-fiction?
  Write F or NF.

  a Sea Creatures   _____

  b Run, Run As Fast As You Can   _____

  c Escape from Mystery Mountain   _____

  d The World's Most Famous Cars   _____

e Learn to Draw _____

f Aliens from the Planet Glurgle _____

g An Encyclopedia of Trees _____

h Hunt for the Silver Sword _____

Practice

2 Number these authors from 1 to 10 to show them in alphabetical order. Use their last names (in **bold**) for the alphabetical order.

2	June **Crebbin**
☐	Pippa **Goodheart**
☐	Thomas **Docherty**
☐	Adam **Stower**
☐	Julia **Donaldson**

☐	Michael **Rosen**
1	Helen **Cooper**
☐	Julia **Jarman**
☐	Nick **Sharratt**
☐	Allan **Drummond**

Watch out!
You might have to look at the third letter in some words to place them in alphabetical order.

Challenge

The Dewey Decimal System

This is how we organise the non-fiction books
in our library.
Look for the numbers on the spines of the books.

000–099	for general subjects
100–199	for philosophy
200–299	for religion
300–399	for social sciences
400–499	for languages
500–599	for science
600–699	for technology
700–799	for art and leisure
800–899	for literature
900–999	for history and geography

3 Using the Dewey Decimal System, write the number section
each of these books would be found in.

a *The Life Cycle of a Frog* _____

b *Religions Around the World* _____

c *The History of America* _____

d *Mobile Phones Today* _____

e *Learning to Draw*   _____

f *Great Children's Authors*   _____

g *Speaking German on Holiday*   _____

h *100 Questions about Space*   _____

› 8.3 Inside a non-fiction book

Language focus

In **non-fictions** texts:

- the **heading** tells you what the topic is
- the **text** gives information about the topic
- if the text is quite long, **subheadings** tell you where the different bits of the topic are talked about
- the **photographs**, **illustrations** and **diagrams** give you information using pictures not words
- a **caption** is a short explanation of what is in a picture
- a **label** names part of a diagram
- some of the information might be given in a **list**, with or without **bullet points**
- there might be a **glossary** to tell you what some of the difficult words mean.

Focus

1 Look at the following page from a book. Label the page with the features in the boxes.

Islands

a _____

b _____

An island is a piece of land that is completely surrounded by water. Some islands are very big while others are small. Islands can be in cold places or in hot places. Some islands have large populations, others are **uninhabited***.
Many islands were formed when volcanoes **erupted***. Examples of volcanic islands include the Canary Islands, such as Tenerife and Lanzarote, and some of the Lesser Antilles islands in the Caribbean Sea.

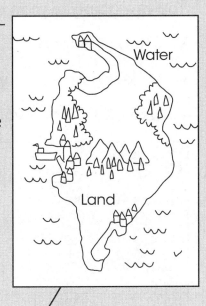

Caribbean islands c _____

d _____

The Caribbean islands are a group of islands in the Caribbean Sea.
They include the islands of:

- Cuba
- Jamaica
- Barbados
- Antigua
- Saint Lucia.

e _____

a beautiful beach in Antigua

f _____

g _____

> **uninhabited:** describes a place with no people living in it
>
> **erupt:** when a volcano erupts molten rock and gases explode from the volcano

Practice

2 You are going to plan a page from a non-fiction book on sport.

- Choose a sport.

- Make notes about your book page using the features in the table.

- Use information you would choose to include on your page.

Heading	
Notes for text	
List	
Diagram	
Caption for diagram	
Subheading	
Glossary	

Challenge

3 Now present your non-fiction book page using the plan you made in **Practice**.

You need to show what information you will place where.
For example, the title will need to go at the top of the page.

> 8.4 Skimming and scanning

Focus

1 Read these questions. <u>Underline</u> the key word or phrases you need information about so you can answer each question.

    a Which <u>types of home</u> are in the <u>centre of the cities</u>?

    b Why might some families live near the edge of the city?

    c Which island has chattel houses on it?

    d Why can chattel houses be moved to different places?

    e How old are the oldest chattel houses?

Practice

2 Scan the information. <u>Underline</u> the key words or phrases you highlighted in **Focus**.

Homes

Cities on Caribbean islands often have new and expensive flats or apartments in the centre. Cheaper houses are normally further out, around the edge of the city.

In Barbados, wooden houses built on stone blocks are called chattel houses. They can be moved to different places because they are not built into the ground. Chattel houses are often painted in pale colours to help keep them cool. The oldest chattel houses were built more than 200 years ago.

Challenge

3 Scan the text to help you answer these questions.

a Which types of homes are in the centre of the cities?

_____

b Why might some families live near the edge of the city?

_____

c Which island has chattel houses on it?

_____

d Why can chattel houses be moved to different places?

_____

e How old are the oldest chattel houses?

_____

> 8.5 Using paragraphs

Language focus

Remember, a **multi-clause sentence** can be made up of two simple sentences joined with a **connective**.

A connective is used to join sentences. Connectives can reflect time, place or cause.

Example:

time connectives	=	first	next	last	then
place connectives	=	up	over	behind	
cause connectives	=	so	if	because	

> **Continued**
>
> We can make paragraphs more exciting by using different types of sentences.
>
> **Conditional sentences** are made up of a main clause and a *conditional* clause. Conditional clauses usually begin with *if* or *unless* and can come before or after the main clause.
>
> **Example:**
>
> I will visit the beach today, **unless** it is raining.
>
> main clause   conditional clause

Focus

1 Complete the sentences with connectives.

    a Some people visit the Caribbean for the holidays _____ other people live there.

    b Tourists enjoy sitting on the beach _____ swimming in the sea.

    c Hurricanes can be dangerous _____ the winds are extremely powerful.

    d People sit in storm shelters, _____ they can find one close-by.

Practice

2 Write your own multi-clause sentence for:

- a time connective

- a place connective

- a cause connective.

a   A time connective

_____

_____

b   A place connective

_____

_____

c   A cause connective

_____

_____

Challenge

3   Complete these sentences as conditional sentences.

   a   I will bring my bike _____.

   b   I will wear a hat _____.

   c   We can finish watching the movie _____.

   d   You get water from ice _____.

> 8.6 Language features of information texts

Language focus

Non-fiction writing includes *facts* and sometimes *opinions*.

A **fact** is something that is known to be true.

An **opinion** is someone's thoughts on something, but it isn't always based on facts.

Focus

1   Tick (✓) the sentences that give opinions.

   a   Have you been to Uluru? It's amazing!

   b   Uluru is one of Australia's best-known geographical features.

   c   Many people enjoy the experience of walking around the base of Uluru.

   d   Uluru is near the Simpson Desert, where the sand is red.

   e   We watched the sun setting at Uluru, which was wonderful.

   f   Uluru was created about 600 million years ago.

   g   Uluru is about 3.6 km long.

   h   Visit Uluru! It's an unforgettable experience!

Practice

2 Write two more sentences about Uluru that could be part of an information text. Use the photograph to help you.

Sentence 1: _____

_____

Sentence 2: _____

_____

Challenge

3 Choose a subject.

a Write two facts about the subject.

Fact 1: _____

Fact 2: _____

b Write two opinions about the subject.

Opinion 1: _____

Opinion 2: _____

> 8.7 Non-fiction e-texts

Focus

1 List three ways e-texts are different to books.

_____

_____

_____

Practice

2 Complete the table of features of printed books and e-texts.
Use the words and phrases in the box.

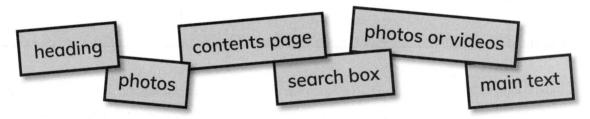

Books	e-texts	Purpose
	drop-down menu	tells you where you can find a topic
	heading	tells you what the topic is

Books	e-texts	Purpose
main text		gives you information
index		helps you to find a particular word or idea
–	hyperlinks	lets you move to other information linked to the topic
		illustrates information so you can see it as well as read about it

Challenge

3 List the advantages of using e-texts compared with books.

_____

_____

_____

_____

4 List the disadvantages of using e-texts compared with books.

_____

_____

_____

_____

› 8.8 Planning a talk

Imagine you have been asked to give a talk on your favourite hobby.

Focus

1 Choose a hobby.

Write three reasons why you think people will find a talk on this hobby interesting.

_____

_____

_____

Practice

2 Write a list of key words you will use in your talk.

Challenge

3   Plan your talk.

Subject:	
Topics and questions	**Answers**

> 8.9 Giving your talk

Focus

1   Think about the work you did on planning and presenting your talk in Sessions 8.8 and 8.9 in the Learner's Book.

What did you do well and what could you have done better?

Give yourself a mark out of 5 for how well you:

- worked in your group ☐

- researched your topic ☐

- presented your research ☐

- listened to others. ☐

Practice

2 Write notes about what you did well and what could you have done better.

Working in a group

I did these things well:

_____

_____

I didn't do these things very well:

_____

_____

Next time I will do these things to make my work even better:

_____

_____

Researching my topic

I did these things well:

_____

_____

I didn't do these things very well:

_____

_____

Next time I will do these things to make my work even better:

_____

_____

Challenge

3 Write notes about what you did well and what could you have done better.

Presenting my research

I did these things well:

_____

_____

I didn't do these things very well:

_____

_____

Next time I will do these things to make my work even better:

_____

_____

Listening to others

I did these things well:

_____

_____

I didn't do these things very well:

_____

_____

Next time I will do these things to make my work even better:

_____

_____

> 8.10 Planning an information text

Read this information text.

India

About India

India is part of the continent of Asia. It is a huge country with a population of well over a billion people. The world's highest mountain range, the Himalayas, borders the north of India. In the southeast is the Bay of Bengal, and in the southwest is the Arabian Sea.

The Himalayas

Geography of India

The land in India is varied. The Thar Desert in the west is dry but the jungles in the northeast of the country are hot and wet. The Ganges Plain, which covers most of northern India, is very fertile so it is a good place to grow crops.

Focus

1 List the interesting and significant words in the information text about India.

Practice

2 List five questions that have been answered in the information text about India.

Question 1: _____

Question 2: _____

Question 3: _____

Question 4: _____

Question 5: _____

Challenge

3   Complete the planning sheet that might have been written before writing the information text about India.

Subject:	
Topics and questions	Answers

> 8.11 Writing an information text

Focus

1 Look again at the information text about India in Session 8.10 and answer these questions.

    a Do many people live in India? Explain your answer.

_____

_____

    b Is India an island? Explain your answer.

_____

_____

    c What is the mountain range in the north of India?

_____

_____

    d Draw lines to match the places on the left with the geographical descriptions on the right.

Himalayas	hot and wet
Thar Desert	fertile
jungles	high
Ganges Plain	dry

Practice

2 Now write four questions on an information text you have written.

Question 1: _____

Question 2: _____

Question 3: _____

Question 4: _____

> If you haven't written an information text, you can use one your have read in a book or on the internet.

Challenge

3 Write answers to your questions.

Question 1: _____

_____

Question 2: _____

_____

Question 3: _____

_____

Question 4: _____

_____

〉 8.12 Improving your text

Focus

1 Complete the lists of irregular verbs in their present and past tense forms.

Present tense	Past tense
have	had
is	
	were
come	
	did
make	
	said
write	
	read
find	
	brought

Practice

2 Read this information text. Find and <u>underline</u> all the verbs.

> ### Animals in India
>
> There is nearly 2000 Bengal tigers in India and about 25 000 Indian elephants. Both these animals were now endangered. That was why many now lived in special protected areas called reserves. Indian culture respect animals. Cows are holy animals and cannot be harmed. Cows wandered freely through the streets of big cities.

Challenge

3 Has the writer used the present tense correctly in the information on Animals in India? Correct any verbs that are in the wrong tense.

9 Laughing allowed

> 9.1 Riddles

Language focus

A **pun** is a play on words. Puns can be found in riddles, jokes and poems and they can make them funny.

Puns use a word that has several meanings or that sounds like another word (homophone). They work because you expect the word to mean one thing but then it turns out to mean something else.

Example:

Why do bees have sticky hair? They use honeycombs!

A honeycomb is something you find in a beehive, but a comb is something you comb your hair with.

Other puns work because you change a word, or part of a word, to sound like another.

Example:

What do you call a dinosaur that's a noisy sleeper?
A bronto-snorus!

Instead of brontosaurus, you have the made-up word bronto-snorous – the snore bit makes you think of someone who snores.

Focus

1 Read these riddles and jokes.

- Tick (✓) the riddles that have puns in them.

- Underline the words that have two meanings or words that have been changed in some way.

☐ a What's a sea monster's favourite food?   Fish and ships!

☐ b What's worse than finding a caterpillar in your salad?   Finding half a caterpillar in your salad!

☐ c Where would you find a prehistoric cow?   In a mooseum!

☐ d Tell me, Captain, how far are we from land?

About two miles, sir.

In which direction?

Downwards!

☐ e Waiter, waiter – I'm in a hurry. Will my pizza be long?

No, madam. It'll be round like everyone else's.

☐ f What has four legs but can't walk?   Two pairs of trousers!

☐ g Waiter, waiter – what kind of soup is this?

It's bean soup, sir.

I don't care what it's been – what is it now?

Practice

2   Write two sentences for each of these words to show the different
    meanings they can have.

a   **bank**

Sentence 1: _____

Sentence 2: _____

b   **can**

Sentence 1: _____

Sentence 2: _____

c   **kind**

Sentence 1: _____

Sentence 2: _____

d   **rock**

Sentence 1: _____

Sentence 2: _____

e   **row**

Sentence 1: _____

Sentence 2: _____

f   **trip**

Sentence 1: _____

Sentence 2: _____

Challenge

3 Write your own riddle with a pun.

You could use one of the words from **Practice** in your riddle.

> 9.2 Wordplay in poetry

Focus

1 Write each of these past tense verbs in a sentence.

a screamed _____

b reflected _____

c wrote _____

d ran _____

Practice

2 Complete the table.

Verb	Present tense	Past tense
to know	they know	they _____
to sleep	I _____	I _____
to drive	she _____	she _____
to give	you _____	you _____
to have	it _____	it _____
to help	we _____	we _____
to feed	he _____	he _____

Challenge

3 Scan these words. (Circle) all the irregular past tense forms you can find.

were	night	third	thud	did	taped
cat	ate	thought	tent	board	packet
out	bought	went	sight	packed	cried
laughed	round	is	found	forgot	put
was	said	sheep	sank		

> 9.3 Funny poems and limericks

> **Language focus**
>
> A **limerick** is a funny poem with five lines.
>
> All limericks have the same rhythm and rhyme pattern.
>
> Lines 1, 2 and 5 rhyme, and lines 3 and 4 rhyme.

Focus

1 Read this limerick aloud. Clap out the rhythm.

> There was an old man of Dumbree,
>
> Who taught little owls to drink tea;
>
> For he said 'To eat mice
>
> Is not proper or nice,'
>
> That amiable man of Dumbree.
>
> *Edward Lear*

Did you know that **amiable** means *having a friendly manner?*

2 List the words that rhyme at the end of each line.

_____ _____ _____

_____ _____

Practice

3 Finish this limerick with your own ideas.

Try to make your words fit the rhythm and rhyme pattern of a limerick.

> There was _____ from Niger,
>
> Who _____ with a tiger;
>
> They went _____
>
> And _____ ,
>
> That _____ from Niger.

Challenge

4 Write your own limerick.

You could write it about yourself and include a place you know.

_____

_____

_____

_____

> 9.4 Calligrams and mnemonics

Language focus

A **calligram** is a poem or word arranged on the page to make a picture or shape. The picture shows the theme of the poem or the meaning of the word.

Drawing the shape of a word can sometimes help you remember how to spell a word or its meaning.

Language focus

A **mnemonic** is a saying that helps you to remember the spelling of a word or a fact.

Example:

because = **b**ig **e**lephants **c**an **a**lways **u**nderstand **s**maller **e**lephants

Focus

1   Look at these calligrams. Think about their shapes.

2 Draw calligrams for these words.

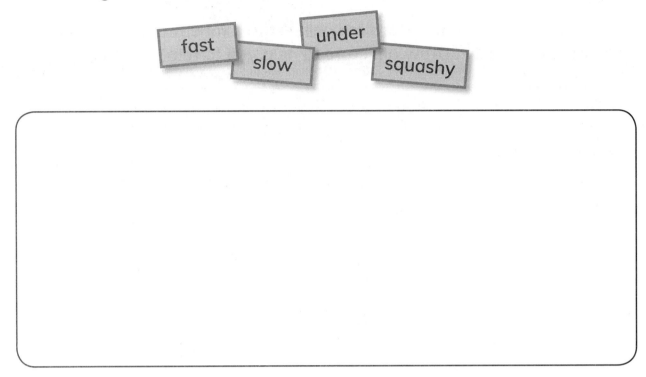

Practice

3 Look at these mnemonics.
   The first letter of each word helps you to spell a word.

   Write the words these mnemonics help you to spell.

   a Rhythm helps your two hips move: _____

   b Big elephants can always understand small elephants:

      _____

   c Only cats' eyes are narrow: _____

   d Not every cat eats sausages (some are really yummy!):

      _____

Challenge

4 Choose a word you find hard to spell. Write a mnemonic to remind you how to spell it. Draw a picture to help you to remember it.

If you can't think of a word, you could try: any, both, have, every, give, many or often.

> 9.5 Reviewing a poem

Focus

1 Look at all the different poems you read in Unit 9.

Wordspinning   The Monster

Whether the Weather   There Was an Old Man with a Beard

Starter   Kite

a   List the poems you found funny.

b   List the poems you found clever.

c List the poems you think were memorable.

> Perhaps you thought
> some of the poems were funny and clever,
> or clever and memorable ... and perhaps
> some of them were all three!

Practice

2 Choose a poem and explain why you found this poem funny, clever and/or memorable.

Poem: _____

_____

_____

_____

_____

_____

Challenge

3 Look at the different sorts of texts you have read in Unit 9.
   Write them where you think they fit best in the diagram.

tongue twisters

riddles

poems with puns

calligrams

funny poems

limericks

mnemonics

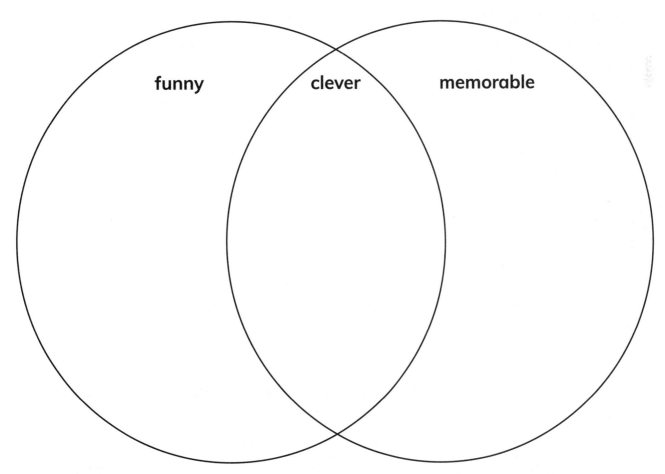

funny   clever   memorable

> 9.6 Writing and performing a poem

Focus

1 Circle the style of poem you want to write.

tongue twister   poem with puns   limerick

riddle   calligram   funny poem

2 Think about what your poem will be about.

Brainstorm your ideas.

Practice

3 Choose five words you might use in your poem, then list three rhyming words for each word you have chosen.

Remember, the words need to rhyme but don't have to have the same spelling pattern, for example, *stairs / bears / hares / shares*.

Word chosen	First rhyming word	Second rhyming word	Third rhyming word

Challenge

4   Look at the style of the poem you have chosen.
    What structure does it have?

5   Using the words in **Practice**, write lines you can
    include in your poem.

    Experiment with different words to see which
    sound the best.

A **calligram**
needs to have a shape.
A **limerick** has five
lines with different
lines rhyming.